LEE

A DRAMATIC POEM

BY

EDGAR LEE MASTERS

CHILDREN OF THE MARKET PLACE

DOMESDAY BOOK

THE GREAT VALLEY

MITCH MILLER

THE OPEN SEA

SKEETERS KIRBY

SONGS AND SATIRES

SPOON RIVER ANTHOLOGY,
    (With Additional Poems)

STARVED ROCK

TOWARD THE GULF

SELECTED POEMS

LEE

A DRAMATIC POEM

BY

EDGAR LEE MASTERS

TO

PERCY GRAINGER

CONTENTS

		PAGE
PROLOGUE	. . . .	1
ACT ONE	. . . .	14
ACT TWO	. . . .	51
ACT THREE.	. . . .	73
ACT FOUR	. . . .	119

LEE

A DRAMATIC POEM

PROLOGUE

The scene is the lawn around the uncompleted Washington monument in the city of Washington. It is in the early morning of April 17th 1861. The air is balmy, the skies fresh and blue through which white clouds are moving amid the glory of vernal sunlight. ORMUND and ARIMANIUS, figures neither old nor young, neither ancient nor modern, but distinguished by something that makes them eternal types, are walking about the monument in earnest talk. They might be Americans of less familiar appearance, or old world characters, but not too alien. The spring wind blows their voices at first before their words become intelligible; and it is evident that they have been in conversation for some time. What is heard at first may be out of the midst of their dialogue, or at the end of it; but it seems to convey the substance of all that they have discussed with each other.

ARIMANIUS

So the talk went while I was listening,
So many voices smote or questioned Him.
They were like noisy suitors round a king,
Or swallows chattering on a fountain's brim.

ORMUND

Our ancient Friend you'd scarcely call a swallow?

1

ARIMANIUS

No, but a falcon bronzed by storm and fire.
He flew the argument where none else could follow
With reasons out of pity, out of ire.

ORMUND

But wanting war?

ARIMANIUS

                    Well, wanting for his side
The victory, and seeing all the good
In the rebel spirit of defeated pride,
This essence is a thing long understood.
Strange that a fatal weakness parallels
The friends of Liberty from the dawn of time:
Her purest souls sink into nameless hells,
And all her champions partake of crime.

ORMUND

Just for the hour, for when the paint is dry,
The blood and tears, the canvas then unrolls
Inevitable beauty for the seeing eye—

ARIMANIUS

Beauty! No wonder since He paints with souls!
They call me evil. What is eviler
Than doctrine such as this? I search in vain
For a deep justice, not a sophister
To justify the tragedy and explain.
Yet if I said—if truth be not for man—
He may use magic to create delight,
And make him beauty, every Puritan

Would brand me as a spirit of the night;
Then in the next breath shout for moral truth,
And rout me in all senates voting war.
Beauty and happiness are the poison blooth
That the victorious deities abhor.
If such the Will be for this little earth,
Then just to spite Him I would have its leaven
Carried above to prove its larger worth,
And see His will on earth be done in heaven.

ORMUND

You must have seen it.   Heaven is all around us,
As round that obelisk swims the April sky.

ARIMANIUS

Perhaps! But its confusing laws confound us,
What is the central truth, and where and why?
From the first day an offering of fruits
And flowers adorned His altar all in vain:
He must have blood and smoking flesh of brutes—
So He respected Abel and not Cain.
So cursed the farmer, made of work a curse
With sweat and hunger, and so cursed the soil;
Yet the Old Falcon might have plotted worse:
The tree of knowledge is the tree of toil.
So toil is good—a better thing might be—
Surely not idleness nor innocence—
To make man but to keep him from the tree
Does meagre credit to omnipotence.
To fashion him from doltish dust but leave him
To wander with the beasts—well, what a world!

He rose to greatness, though the rise aggrieve him—
I'm glad the snake around the tree was curled.
He rose through disobedience and is blest
By thoughts and understandings for the sin;
But still the disobedience is assessed
In loss and anguish as their origin.
So the two currents in the fathomless stream;
And even to this troubled hour they flow:
An offering of fruits and flowers seem
Rejected for a people's loss and woe.
The South is Cain, the farmer, doing ill,
Whose offering to heaven is nothing worth.
Cornered and angered he designs to kill,
And Abel's voice is crying from the earth.
The ground is cursed and trodden on by Steel,
Commerce and Cities chant the cursing song
Of Cain the farmer. So the iron heel
Will bring disaster to undo a wrong
Used for its studied purpose to conceal
Its tireless machinations for the strong.

ORMUND

Let it be so. Let tares and wheat be sown:
By your own word the tares will all be known,
Since man had vision eating the forbidden
Fruit of the tree. And if the ground be cursed
With blood, from man the curse will not be hidden—
The path of higher life will be traversed.
The law's injunction is a broken tooth:
Earth has no garden, no forbidden tree;
Who but His Son told us to seek the truth?

Who told us that the truth would make us free?
But who can grant remission of the pain
Which must attend the toil, the life defeat?

ARIMANIUS

That is the failure making all our gain
So little, when it might be all so sweet.
Now all the heavens are torn with mad debate;
Voices surround us, even now I hear them:
Goodness enforced degenerates to hate
Through doctrines urged on souls who can't revere them.
The old Book may be used to free the slave,
If you ignore the slavery it taught.
But freeing him it will again deprave
The emancipating minds who live its thought.
We two perceive the years that will ensue
Of cruel wrong, injustice, tyranny.
A Book that is not wholesome through and through
Is scarce the product of divinity.

ORMUND

So is it with man who plays an evil part
With bigotry as a devil in his heart.

ARIMANIUS

Now all the talk is violence and God,
Superior virtue and superior brawn.
And this same crew with this unloosened rod
Of lawless sovereignty will make a pawn
Of isles beneath the Spainard's beck and nod,
And slave a brown race ere the century's dawn—

These who are praying that the press be trod,
And His swift terrible sword again be drawn.

ORMUND

That John Brown's soul may still go marching on.

ARIMANIUS

Yes, but no farther than the pulpit spouters
Who fled to Europe when the scamp was hung.
Of their own creed they are at last the doubters,
Their faith and courage lie upon the tongue.
They gathered funds for him for insurrection
In Kansas, which he did not lead and then
He came to Harper's Ferry where detection
Laid hands upon his treason and his men.

ORMUND

Well, but you know the boasting prophecy
In earth and heaven in the name of Brown:
His rebel soul shall hunt the rebel Lee,
And Harper's Ferry track rebellion down.

ARIMANIUS

This I would stave. But break my heart at last
If death come not, but malice to amerce
Life that is spared Lee, that he may be cast
To shame and torture as a daily curse.
Quick blood for him, sweet swooning and the press
Of Hastings' shadows or from Runnymede.
O, lyric bullet of the Wilderness
Give him sweet requiem—let his bosom bleed!

Come quickly, angel brother, stoop and kiss
Nobly the brow that is nobility.
Let the cause perish, but no cowardice
Soil him when freeman are no longer free;
When the triumphant bigots with their gods
Howl over ruins, cities lapped with flames,
Let him not sit in stocks amid the nods
Of thieves and cut-throats railing out their shames.

ORMUND

Yet he shall live.

ARIMANIUS

Such evils to endure?

ORMUND

Heroically—immortalized by Duty.
Not you alone move to the mystic lure;
The Soul above all souls must have its beauty.
The world seeks, and its races, seek the ages
For gems fire fused, compacted by the rocks
Of great disaster; and the value gauges
By what survives the crushes and the shocks.
So if the soul of Brown pursue and take
The soul of Lee in battle cannon waged,
His marches farther who shall not forsake
The vision while an erring people raged.
'Tis better that one die and not the many,
There must be sacrifice if the people live—

ARIMANIUS

Let them pay tribute with a Cæsar penny—

ORMUND

They triumph who go forward and forgive.
Brown arms the great revenge and dies therefor.
The slaves are freed and other men are slaved;
But Lee for independence wages war,
Only by beauty are a people saved,
And by the truth of least alloy of metal
Corroding at the day's end when it's coined;
Time leaves no debt that Life escapes to settle,
Pay fully is the rule of old enjoined . . .
What vexed the world in 1761?
The Bourbon compacts, capture of Belle-Isle;
The Earl of Bute, Turgot, the Austrian
Making Silesia his domicile;
And Pondicherry taken at last by Coote;
And Paris listening to Diderot;
If soon passed out the ministry of Bute
The world still had Voltaire, and had Rousseau.
And Otis in this land against the writs
Of customs seizing smuggled steel and silks—
Shudder! A shadow before our vision flits,
Named for the English red republican Wilkes.

ARIMANIUS

I see it. Men are ignorant when they ask
To know the future; 'tis enough to see
The past, and trembling bend beneath the task
Of solving what the present even may be.
But to see all, and on the sky unroll
At will the past, and what is yet to come,

That is the blood sweat of the fainting soul
Who knows not what it means, and so is dumb.
Sound waves of every voice that ever spoke,
Or speaks this moment fill the magic air,
I hear them: that was Calas' when they broke
His body on the wheel; and Robespierre
Moans as they take the bandage from his jaw;
And Jackson now says, "Let us cross the river,"
And Burns who asks again for usquebaugh.
What has been said reverberates forever,
What will be said with finer energy
Stirs and we hear it—

ORMUND

                    List that voice of words:
Government of the people still must be,
Nor ever fail, nor perish from the earth—

ARIMANIUS

His who inhabits yonder storied hall,
Where Jefferson the democrat abode!

ORMUND

His fame shall be more sounded than them all.

ARIMANIUS

Yet he's the blossom of one episode,
Whose bud is Union, he is not a root
Which feeds the trunk and branches and the buds
With life to every tendril, leaf, volute.

Union may be for liberty if it floods
With vital dew the roots spread far below,
Of Locke, Lorenzo, More, the great Virginian;
Or it may feed the banyan tree to grow
Over the land with darkening dominion.
The heavens must not be hidden, nor the land
Devoured and tangled—let the Union be;
But still resistance is the fruitful hand
Which trims and tends the growth of Liberty.
Shall the hand falter under hateful force,
Or tire for thickets hindering its power?
Union will then be but the intercourse
Of gormand trunks whose hunger is their flower.
What matter if his rise was from the ranks,
What the log cabin, and the river trails,
As a youth he was for privilege and the banks
Now fortressed by a block-house of fence rails.
Union he gives us. Will it match the gift
Of will for independence, will it match
The Liberty discarding every shift,
The flag fresh woven without seam or patch?
Mt. Vernon, Monticello rising above
Will it ennoble? This is understood:
The truth must be beloved or else the love
Brings evil to annul its promised good.

(*They walk to the base of the Washington Monument.*)

ORMUND

The unfinished truncate of this obelisk
Is sky anhungered!

ARIMANIUS

A work too long delayed:
Like independence fearful of the risk,

ORMUND

Or Liberty that steps aside for Trade.
Hereafter it shall take a star for beacon
Up pointed from this base where Webster spoke—

ARIMANIUS

I hope its symbol spirit will not weaken—
He was a willow tree who seemed an oak.
He was the voice of Hamilton whose magic
Makes ruling fasces of the woodman's ax.
I am a devil with a spirit tragic
For simple eyes and for believing backs.

ORMUND

Yet there shall be a monument of grandeur
Surpassing this, for him who rules to-day;
Nor acid truth, analysis, nor slander
Shall ever waste its lofty stones away.

ARIMANIUS

And what for Lee?   Let's to the river walk.
There stands his Arlington his sorrow housing.
The child of Washington is a troubled stalk
Amid these storms of war so loud carousing.
He is in prayer, and through the night has prayed.
What shouts and curses coursed around his prayer.
If men could know, as we, the madness weighed
In the thin balance of the listening air.

ORMUND

He shall drink from the cup of dark despair.

ARIMANIUS

Yes, I forsee. His branches shall be riven
And cast to earth in sorrow and defeat;
Yet they shall nourish earth, and smiling heaven
Shall bless the grass lands and the fields of wheat.
If no great plan of his shall ever flourish,
No victory, nor ultimate campaign,
His duty done from day to day shall nourish,
Like the crushed harvest of the yearly grain.
What laurel leaves shine as the maize's blades?
What vine fruit like the hard but golden seeds?
What wintered oak sees not as winter fades
The annual harvest as the snow recedes?
So men live by the food of daily deeds
Grown out of duty done to aid the Plan
Sensed at the heart in selfless faith and creeds—
Who can serve God? But who cannot serve man?

ORMUND

John Brown of Ossawatomie will never
With his rebellion vanquish such a Lee.

ARIMANIUS

Then let his soul go marching on forever
Behind Lee's in the van of Liberty.
Let the specific love that uses hate
Have its reward, though much it interferes
With Love and Liberty—

ORMUND

The larger Fate
Has minutes on its dial marked in years.
Let's cross the river, round his mansion stroll
And nearer drawing bring our wisdom to him—

ARIMANIUS

Even it seems you love this troubled soul.

ORMUND

I see the Fates that ruin and renew him.
(They cross the river to Arlington.   The scene closes.)

ACT ONE

The scene: A chamber in Arlington.   Lee is alone.

LEE

My prayers avail me little, yet I pray.
Asking for clearer light, if such there be.
No fuller light is granted, yet I pray.
There was the inner voice which uttered Duty,
Then ceased, now speaks no more;
And by that single utterance left in fear
The heart that heard, and dared the less to fail,
Being unrestrained,
Save for that voice, grown silent, and whose silence
Is stronger than its tongue.
My Duty! Which the inner eye beheld
At the first.   Oh, did I see aright?
And now with gazing on the face I saw
Have I stared down its truth?
And are its waning lineaments
My eyes, or its reality?
If the great Power would sustain me now!
Inform, direct, and lift me to highest truth!
If the Maker of the soul,
And knower of its secrets, which are deeper
Than life's re-births, or the laws of moving worlds
Would reveal to me

14

The path that I should take,
So to fulfill what He would have fulfilled,
So rightly to perform the task assigned me
In this thick tangled plot of men and days!
I do not fear calamity, no nor death.
The human soul should equal human woe:
For He has made it strong.
My fear is only, if I err,
And work against His plan, and be a stumbling
To His predestined ordering of the world;
And a falsehood in its story, and a note
That mars its harmony.
Yet there may be
A music higher, equal it may be,
To the chorus of the triumph, the acclaim
Of angels for the end that was designed.
But if true glory, honor, be not his
Who serves his vision, works his duty through;
And only glory, honor, come to him
Who sees aright, and serves aright,
Then I would know this hour
Some other path than Duty, as my eyes,
Wakeful and straining now no other see.
I would be lifted from the course
Where I must ask forgiveness, come to sight.
I would be made a trumpet, tuned by the eternal laws
Of great events, for the country I adore,
And hailing the glory of God, and the rightful cause
For the world's emerging fate.
I would not be an object of eternal bounty,
Forgiven, but adjudged as in the wrong,

And at the best accepted as a note
Which makes the strain of other souls more true,
Being a harshness among men, and to my land
The sound of barbarous kettles, though to God
A needed strophe for the symphony.
Not this, save I be equal, and as loved
As those attuned.
But if I am a trump not to be blown
True to the triumphant chord;
And if in God's omniscience some are born
To vision of His vision,
And nerved with resolution to obey it,
And gifted thus are His anointed sons
For the world to hear and live by;
While some are born with vision which mis-sees,
But nerved no less with strength to do,
And I am one, then I would know this,
So to go forth to sorrow and defeat,
And mortified rejection by the fate
Which moulds as God decrees,
Sustained by Him in faith that duty done
Is glory, and is made acceptable
By the mystical grace of Christ,
And ranged with Wisdom, Goodness. Thus I pray!
For even my defeat may be the lifting
Of the world of spirits and truth!

                          (Mrs. Lee enters.)

MRS. LEE

Do you still struggle Robert? Is the truth
So hard to find, to hold, that all the night

You needs must pray and seek? The boisterous wind
Which all these hours has roared the budding trees,
And skimmed the river of the April stars
Has quieted and sleeps; and morning birds
Begin to twitter. I have lain awake,
And suffered for the springs whose ghosts do wail
At the solemn loveliness of this spring,
Which finds our hearts so torn, our home so rent.
Still sleeps my kinsman, and your kindred soul,
His life and labors done—how in the spring
We think of those long dead! And now of him,
Seeing our country's peril, and the strife
That storms about us, do I think of him,
By day, by night. And all this night I saw
These waters dream and glide beside the tomb
Which stands upon Mt. Vernon, round whose roofs
The birds of dawning sing . . . and still he sleeps.
While all the world has changed, and war awakes
Among his sons, who should be friends, and whom
He counseled to peace. But he, though sleeping,
Speaks to his countrymen, to you . . . O hear!

LEE

With my soul's agony I have sought
His counsel, as before
Through all my life, have I in trials and doubts
Looked to him as my guide, more in this hour.
For in this instant problem
Have I had wonder what his course would be.
So in the darkness of this hour I look
Into his life to find the truth for mine. . . .

His state, my state, has riven the covenant
Which bound it to the others. Shall I stand
For or against Virginia? If against
Do I not desecrate the soil where rests
Your kinsman, and the soul by whom my life
Was fashioned from the first, even as a boy?
He fought to break the bands which bound Virginia
To England, and to give Virginia station
Separate and equal among the Powers of earth,
The sovereignty of her people won.
She delegated sovereign powers, not sovereignty,
To the Union which he formed, and now withdraws
The granted powers. And this is revolution,
But revolution without blood, save they assail us,
Invade us, and so shed it. If they do
Shall I be of the forces which assail,
The shedders of my people's blood?
Or shall I draw my sword in their defense,
And if I draw it do I follow him,
Or do him violence?
Is revolution evil, is it good,
In man's determination, or does God
Make the same thing an evil or a good,
As pleases Him, and doing so make use
For His own glory of men, and so of me?
Yet what I see is this: the South withdraws
For civil liberty, not slavery!

MRS. LEE

How will it stand in history? Oh be sure!

LEE

God is a God of truth.

MRS. LEE

And if this be the truth, and hidden from you?

LEE

I have prayed, and I have striven.
I have no part in human slavery.
I hate it for its slavery of us,
And for its palsying hand, and for its soiling.
It is a dying growth, and cannot last,
However end the war. So much the worse
A war to end it, if the war be such.
But there is slavery more odious
Than the bonded black:
It is that slavery which the North essays
To fasten on us now, by war begun
By them, not us; and by the moral trick
Of bringing food to Sumter, which must needs
Provoke resistance.

MRS. LEE

Oh, but these cries from Ossawatomie,
These songs, these shouts, these prayers!

LEE

And so they do what Brown did,
Whom Lincoln censured, saying
His crime was of the gravest.
Now Lincoln makes a virtue in an army
Of what was crime in Brown.

MRS. LEE

And yet my woman's mind
Perceives reality more strong in this
Than thought perceives.

LEE

But who shall speak?   Their Lincolns or their Browns?
Their Lincoln has avowed no will to end
Or interfere with slavery.   So it is
Not war about the slaves, nor do I war
To keep, defend the curse.
The issue is self-government
Against the hand of Lincoln, who proclaims
His purpose to possess the forts, not theirs,
But ours, since we have sovereignty resumed
Over the land that holds them.
And if this Union, that I loved, must fall;
This Union that my Washington bequeathed,
Because its soul has fled, and is no more
The Union of my Washington, what is left
But Union newly made of states, which build
Greatly upon the truths the North belies?

MRS. LEE

If it may be against that populous North
Of ships and engines, rails and factories,
And coal and steel and corn,
And millions overtopping us in arms!

LEE

The God of battle can sustain us,
As he sustained our Washington who warred

Against an England mightier than the North.
But what's my part, whatever be the end?
Virginia is my country, I obey
Her will, whatever be my fate!
If war must be, and we be overwhelmed,
God is a God of righteousness no less;
And a new nation may come forth
Chastened, and strengthened, happier than the old,
And happier than the one the South designs.
This falsehood that the war is waged to free
The slave, may in the working of the Muse,
Who writes what men arise by and so live by,
Become a truth, and by creative glory
Lead to new liberty, and happiness.
If I am but an arm that balks the forces
Arising to sweep down decay and wreck,
And cleanse for this domain of future hope;
If I am but an instrument which stays
For a time the gathered waters, and so augment
The irresistible strength of Time, until they burst,
And flood and bear away
All wastage and debris, and even myself,
Leaving the people clean
Of death, decay and perished days;
If my part played in duty, make a war
More terrible and prolonged, which must be so
To sweep and flame and purge,
And save for my resistance would not be,
Have I not served the will of God as much
As if he crowned my labors for the South
With victory for the South, and by that will

Made good the path of paths innumerable
Which God can choose for good? For nothing is
Save God decrees it, neither their acts nor mine;
And we should ask forgiveness who condemn
The souls of different thought, our foes,
Whose deeds must be of God, and make the sum
Of history and fate.
One thing is ours, to watch and pray,
And hear the voice of Duty, our only guide!

MRS. LEE

Oh, but our lives, our happy lives, our lives
Lived to this day in honor and in peace!
This Arlington, our home, that came to us
From Washington, my kinsman! This great hall,
Perched on this sunny eminence, amid our trees,
Above this river, where our daily eyes
Have seen the capitol, and the flag, you swore
To serve, defend, obey!
This birthplace of our children, and these rooms;
This lawn where they have played!
This spot of hospitality, and feasts;
This loveliness to leave, and to descend
To the valleys of fear, the wastes of loneliness,
And poverty, it may be!
I have dreamed it out, have thought it through.
And even to-night I dreamed that all was lost:
Your station, peace of mind; and this, our home,
And all its acres had been seized and made
A plot of burial for the northern dead,
Whose countless headstones dappled the shadowed sward

Under this moon.
Thus by intolerable irony were you,
My husband seared and branded, for all time;
And the ghosts of those who fell, because you fought,
Were loosened here to wail about these walls,
And on these walks where you and I have strayed,
You were cursed, while the idle multitudes
Of future days were free to pass this door,
And say with scornful gestures: "Here he lived!"
It should not be: You who from a boy
Have led the blameless life,
Fulfilling the brave blood of Harry Lee,
And that great man who spoke and wrought for truth,
Your kinsman Richard Henry.
It should not be: You the good son,
The faultless student, and the gifted captain,
Honored for Mexico, and honoring
Your country's war!
It should not be, my husband, perfect heart
To my weak woman's heart; and perfect father
To our little brood that sleeps, while we stare out
With prayers and tears the midnight. O, my husband,
My adored, think of yourself, if not of us,
And of our home!
Think if this loathsome serpent slavery,
This thing of stings and fangs,
Be not intent on use of you,
To take the splendor of your name, your skill,
For its insatiable hunger, as even now,
It has devoured the South, and is not full.
You have declined the North's command; so be.

Resign if need be your commission too,
And let us live.
But never draw your sword against the North:
It will be written that against the Union
You drew your sword.   And thus to loss of home,
Fortune and friends, and fame that might be yours,
If you should lose—but I have dread to speak. . . .

LEE

You mean my honor?

MRS. LEE

Your honor, Robert.
Slander is many tongued.
Forgive me other reasons: first your age.
You are no more the youth of Cerro Gordo,
The prime vitality of Chapultepec.
And will you bear the marching, and the waking,
The strife, and envy?   Envy too will come.
How will your tenderness endure the cries,
The still white faces of the youths you lead?
You who were moved so by the little girl
Who wept in Mexico for a brother slain?
Besides my woman's eyes behold such trifles
As dust on tattered banners, to depress
The people you would thrill, and win, whose hopes
Want bright and buoyant flags and sunny skies. . . .
There will be rain and hunger. . . .

LEE

Always so.

MRS. LEE

And the deep misfortune of intolerable death
To captains on whom you lean.

LEE

Or of myself on whom all captains lean.

MRS. LEE

Then who will lead the South?
And to your death
There will be added conquest of your cause,
And the silence that will cover your intent,
And these your purest prayers, and sifted will,
And conscience weighed and tested!

LEE

No, I have faith in God.
And though He slay me, still will I believe.
His children never know the second death:
To be miswritten forever, or lost in air,
Which hides their faith and love.
Still rings within my ears my father's words:
Virginia is my country.   And still shines
The faith of Washington, who had to meet
All that confronts me now:
The loss of fortune, fame, and a traitor's fate,
If he should fail!
But if the soul could stand, life be at rest,
Then might I sit at home, and keep our home,

Which breaks your heart to lose.
But life will stay not, and there is in man
That which in waking and in sleep still stirs,
And says, Press forward! Onward!
Bring me the noon hour, and the afternoon;
Bring me the night, and bring again to-morrow,
Till no to-morrows be, and the soul's era change!
Bring me the better work, the fitter task,
The destiny that is mine, and not these shifts
Of substitute days!
The soul seeks consummations, must have blossom
For the meaningless growth of the stalk,
If never blossom be.
And as the spirit of the seed is sighing
For the sprout, for the blade, the ear,
And fears not burial, and its own decay
To reach these hopes,
So the soul of man is fated by the urge
Of life, the gift of God;
And in its will, that cannot be denied,
Nor hushed, nor put aside,
To be sown, and so to achieve,
Confronts disaster as its burial;
And looks to death as life, and as the goal
To which life moves along the tangled path
Of little and daily living and events,
Parted and pushed aside and trampled down,
To reach reality, the last and best!
Disaster is more welcome than decay;
And the running brook that plunges and is lost
In the devouring deeps, has life above the pond

That greens in lethargy and saves itself.
Here am I now at middle age, and more;
And by these comforts eased into decline.
Is this my soul's end, this the meaning of life?
If it were conscience only, not the urge
Of the soul, may I say God, could I repose,
And drift in this serene calm of days?
But rather since in the flesh of conscience crackles
The ferment which must sour, or come to wine,
I have no choice except to act—but how?
Where my belief is, or my belief is not?
Against my people, my Virginia?
Or for my people, my Virginia?
For Liberty, and for the creed that means
A liberty for all?   Or to strike down
The creed whose ruin means the despotism
Which Washington and Jefferson foretold?
No, it must be!   This sword which I had hoped
Never to draw again, must be unsheathed
To sustain what I most deeply love.
And since I cannot choose but act,
It must be with the South, and not the North!

MRS. LEE

And yet you weep, so saying—and I weep.
Failure, dishonor to your blood and life
Do not belong.
Your heritage forbids, your course, your gifts;
Your ordered life, your heroship, your truth,
Formed by your great exemplars.
Some there have been whose final act of life

Has been the fitting exposition of their play.
But for you, my Robert, after these gracious days,
This great esteem, this honor, this success,
To come to days of torment, to the flies
And hornets of exasperate life;
To contempt, it may be, and to your written name
Upon the list of traitors and betrayers;
To failure, and worst tragedy of all
To hatred in old age! O, terrible fate!
And if at last God should forsake you,
And the light in you should be made darkness,
And the windows of faith should be darkened,
Oh, what a night for your soul!

LEE

Even as He wills, so let it be.
But now my eye is single, and all my thought
Is full of light!

MRS. LEE

Would it were so! And would He stay
The hands that seek to cast you like a pearl
Amid the mire, when you should be kept,
Cherished and worn, a treasure beyond price,
And a beauty to your countrymen forever!

LEE

Who are my countrymen that I shall not be so,
If I perform my duty?
Each must resolve that peace, self-government,

And liberty in him shall have a friend,
And a defender to the death.
My soul is fixed, and with the dawn, which comes,
And lightens now the earth, my eyes are cleared.

(He writes.)

MRS. LEE

What do you write?

LEE

Virginia has my sword!   What was that sound?

MRS. LEE

Our waking children laugh!

(She leaves the room weeping.   Lee kneels in prayer.)

LEE

Now I have gone the round of life,
And all is known
Of wife and children, home,
And wars that came to peace,
And settled fruitage.
Now all is known, save what lies in the darkness
Of days to be,
Toward which my soul moves, driven forth
By the emptiness of days that were.
Now all is known, save the darkness of the soil,
Wherein the soul descends that it may leaf
And prosper days made new.
Now all is known, save death,

Which calls me, and I go
To search, to know, and to complete my course.
Sustain me Lord, and guide me.

(The scene closes.)

Scene 2: ORMUND and ARIMANIUS who have been
loitering near the Arlington Mansion listening
to Lee in prayer and in his struggle, now turn
away, and look toward the city of Washington.

ARIMANIUS

Poor soul! His agony would move a stone.
If deeds were children of the heart's intent
Good would attend his course and good alone.

ORMUND

But deeds are children, therefore different
From the begetting wills—there's more than one.
Strains enter the conceptions all unknown.
You may be sure a bad intent begets
An evil consequence, as you may be sure
A good intent the devil himself besets—
Only the blood of evil courses pure.

ARIMANIUS

Then God Himself's the ruling evil doer.

ORMUND

Oh, that's not all the deviltry, as you know:
A bad intent rots down the act that's good:

Self motives, power or money, praise infect;
But good intent as well results in woe.
Men are like children lost in a tangled wood
Whose hope to escape the shadows misdirect.

ARIMANIUS

Yes, and all punishments so much exceed
The magnitude and nature of the deed:
A misplaced love through long and shameful years
May vine and stem and cast proliferate seed,
And multiply in nameless ways its tears.
I have seen evil with unerring aim
Pierce through the hearts of sons of evil sires;
And mercy rarely warm with tender flame
The thousands who respect His hard desires.
Whether you build or wreck to better build
The good stone badly used no less offends;
At last the righteous purpose being unskilled
Brings fallen walls on kindred and on friends.

ORMUND

So Lee may purge his floor of dust and chaff,
Clotho will spin and Lachesis will laugh;
And no nephalia offered will appease
The serpents coifing the Eumenides.
Thousands in peace and happiness to-day,
Farm boys and students in the spring rejoicing
For his ideal devotion soon will pay
Upon the battle-field their sorrow voicing.

ARIMANIUS

These little puffs of air about our cheeks
Bespeak them! From the quiet heavens' fastness!
Whether an army shouts, a drummer shrieks
These zephyrs lisp indifference out of vastness.
Oft in a lonely meadow I have felt them;
To me they whisper men in work or play
Unconscious of the ruin to be dealt them,
The inexorable Shapes that look for them as prey.

ORMUND

Yet all is law, its logic and its sway:
The building falls obedient to a law,
And friends are killed for being in the way.
The dike is answerable for the little flaw
That lets the sea upon a people's bread.

ARIMANIUS

Let us now dim the lights by which we view
The reels' continuous picturing what's ahead.
The distant mists make every falsehood true
And beautiful—there let us gaze instead.
Not Vicksburg now, not Shiloh, nor the dew
Upon the brows of Pickett's glorious dead.

ORMUND

Look! The Republic lifts her awful head.
Come, let us hear her wrath and reasons through.
    (*They leave Arlington and cross the river to the lawn
    about the Washington monument. The scene closes.*)

Scene 3: Near the base of the Washington monument.

THE REPUBLIC

I

1

Destiny, named also God, breathed once again
  Upon the waters and the deeps of life;
And hunger of the body stirred in men
Adventure, before the soul of man in strife
And loneliness of seas, and fears and prayers
   To deaf and dying gods awoke to new
   Visions and hopes more true.
The sea beckons, and Iceland thrills and dares,
And Vinland of wineberries and of wheat
Lures Ericsson.   But seeds for centuries kept
Were the wise dreams of Eratosthenes,
And Aristotle, steering western seas
Till India were reached.   And these had slept
Deep in the narrowing earth of human wants
Two thousand years, when Toscanelli rose
And gave Columbus strength, against the taunts
Of disbelief, who sailed and found
The hemisphere of my domain.
Then Cabot stood upon the very ground
Of my new continent; Balboa for the gain
  Of quickly garnered gold
Mounted the Cordilleras, and returned
Empty, rebellious, though as God had planned
He gave him the Pacific to behold,
And me its waters around my teeming land.

2

Questing for gold and silver, and for bread
Magellan circled the world and Drake;
And by the self-same passion led
The northern coast, to Florida was spread
    Before my eyes; and where the waters break
    By Coronado; and where the Oregon
Roars to the sapphire silence of sky pasturing pines;
    And where the Mississippi waters the Ethiop soil
    Made for me by the glaciers, the giant snails
    Who bore within their shells the vast designs
        Of corn and coal and oil,
        And iron, richer by the added toil
    Of man than gold; and where the wintry gales
    Of the Lakes, of Illinois, Ohio, Michigan,
        Harden the flesh and brighten the eyes
Of the millions later mine under those favorable skies;
        And where the great West and the prairies span
    To the mountains of snow, the sleepless enterprise
    Of tillers builded, as the Artisan
        Of my great life decreed, and still decrees.

II

Then Destiny, named God, breathed once again,
    And gave the children of men
Souls that were new, to English, French and Dutch,
To Scotch and Irish, Germans, in the clutch
Of despot days and girded circumstance.
These like wild birds, who fly exhausted stores
Where the hunters gather, swarmed from wearied France,
From restless England, Scotland, to the shores

Soon to be mine.   And by the sealed device
Of Destiny made Virginia through a weed;
And made the South through cotton and through rice,
And slaves; and made the New World through the law
Which kills, and must be killed if men be free.
Yet ere it hardened and grew lifeless, Fate
Saw Conscience made emancipate,
And man the individual made
The object of devotion, not the State.
Which joined to needs material and to trade
Wrote charters, those of Windsor, Wethersfield,
And Albany where Franklin wrought; at last
The Declaration of my Jefferson,
And the great kinsman of my faltering Lee;
And Henry, who divined this land as one
People and one Faith and Destiny!

III

Thence from those days arose
My strength unto the woes
Of this day's peril, bitter for my soul.
And three score years have seen
Fields turn from gray to green
Since he who prayed for me fell into sleep,
Lulled where Potomac's waters seaward roll.
And still great numbers of my people keep
My stern commandments.   What Balboa sought,
And found not, has been found; and factions pause,
Seeing that gold and trade create the soul
Of foreign friendship, though they make the laws
Which cramp the man, while my domain is wrought.

I look upon the sea Balboa stared,
And hold the river sailed by Cartier;
And rule where Coronado went astray,
And in the West where Clark and Lewis fared.
I lifted Jackson to behold me:
He saw my eyes' light on his sword,
And ruled no power should withhold me
From tuning States to one harmonious chord;
Making one freedom for one realm,
One people, and one helm
For growth and strength, and for the sovereign word.
And as great riches from the mountains poured
From the fields, the forests and the streams,
Won by the lusty émigrés, whose dreams
Found rich fulfillment in a massed
Democracy, I grew in unity;
And from my fingers cast
The manacles, that left to fancy free
The colonies, becoming states at last!
Out of Virginia came the giants
Washington, Marshall to my aid,
Who cleared the pathway of defiance
Of every spirit retrograde.
Nature sustained me by the favorable heat
Of summer and winter sun;
And gave the victory to corn and wheat,
And fabrics forged and spun.
Nature is God, therefore I came of God!
God is desire and thought, and moved the hand
Of Carroll, who the Declaration signed;
Then drove the spike which shod

With rails for steam the land.
Nature is God, and left the South to blind
Her soul with slavery and stagnant life;
While Michigan, Wisconsin, fed my mind
With changing dreams and fruitful strife.
My South is memory living in the past,
Before whose eyes the Present files unknown;
A clock, whose hands are stayed, where a lounger dreams
That noon is, since light is, though noon is flown.
My South is pride, and chivalry, old belief,
Whose roots are in the letter, which misdeems
The truth unchanged.   She rots upon a reef
Where the dead airs of tropic waters die.
My South is like those lazy sisters fed
By sisters who arise at dawn to ply
Their hands about the house that shelters all,
And who by thrift have gained the mastery
Of wealth the loungers used not, nor could use. . . .
So be it.   And so be the weak cabal
Of Envy cursed, and so be Slavery
Cursed and uprooted; be the fatal news
Of this my resolution, and the lists
Of those who fall, by lightning heralded,
Which my great North has taught to fly its wrists.
Be wild protest, and be the moaning dead
As a trumpet trampled under foot; and my surprise
As a flood upon a sleeping town; and be my swords
As the rays of the rising sun, to make as gourds
Of autumn under vines, the whiteness of their bones,
Until my beauty be as mountains of snow
Which the traveler sees afar, and Time shall know

That Force is Right until the strength
Of Truth o'ermasters Force at length.
If Revolution be of God, its overthrow
Must be of God; and like opposing forces
Of nature, recreates for conqueror,
And for the conquered, life with fresh resources.
The South rebels, and heaven decrees the War!

IV

Therefore since some must rule, and some obey;
And God has willed it so, no less than God
Made it the law for masters and for slaves;
And since my southern daughters tear away
My great authority, with an iron rod
They shall be broken, and I give their graves,
And their inheritance to my loyal brood,
The sisters called well-minded, out of dread.
And to this end I call New England first.

NEW ENGLAND

Be ended our long feud.
Until the resurrection of the dead
Be their disloyalty accursed.

THE REPUBLIC

New York!

NEW YORK

The die is cast:
Be Hamilton avenged at last.

ACT I]   LEE: A DRAMATIC POEM   39

THE REPUBLIC

Pennsylvania!

PENNSYLVANIA

Franklin awakes, who gave his eagle soul
To man born free!

THE REPUBLIC

I call upon the whole
States of the Northwest by my ordinance
Barred of this curse.

THE NORTHWEST

           We seize the circumstance
To cleanse the stench with fire, and put at ease
The time-worn strife of hostile sovereignties.
Lincoln is of us, who was suckled on
The faith of Marshall and of Hamilton.
And Douglas who submerges self and life
To save the Union, and to heal its strife.

THE REPUBLIC

Kentucky, Tennessee!

KENTUCKY, TENNESSEE

           Your unutterable
And infamous crusade of hell,
Be hurled to hell!

THE REPUBLIC

Virginia! . . . What no voice?
Neither Westmoreland, no nor Stratford House?
Have they no sons succeeding to espouse
My cause? And do the ivied halls rejoice
Where law and war are taught? Does Lexington,
Her youths, preceptors hate me? Charlottesville
Assemble to defeat my will?
Virginia! Tell me! Now I need my son,
Whose great progenitor at Hastings fought;
Whose kinsman for my institutions wrought;
Whose father Lighthorse Harry was my pride;
Whom I have nurtured for my need to be
In hours like this, to battle at my side;
Where is my soldier son, my Robert Lee?

LEE

Alone!

THE REPUBLIC

Did you not hear me
As one who walked in the garden in the cool
Of the day and called you?

LEE

No, a voice at the pool,
Who cleared my eyes, I heard. May he be near me
To guide me and my soul possess.
I have resolved, but know my nakedness
All men shall see!

THE REPUBLIC

> Unsay!   My armies lead!
> Stand by me in my need.
> Honor I gave you, but a greater give.
> Fame now is yours, you shall have greater fame.
> You shall be endlessly the brightest name
> Lettered upon my annals; you shall live
> As reverenced as Washington, full of years,
> Enriched by great obedience, fervent love. . . .
> Do you despise these for a cause whereof
> No victory can be?

LEE

> I give up all!

THE REPUBLIC

> For what?

LEE

> My duty is imperial!
> I cannot draw my sword against my state,
> Against my kinsman, children and my home!
> Be to me then whatever is to come,
> Whatever of disaster or of fate!
> This is the blood my sire to me bequeathed,
> Whose sword for Revolution was unsheathed,
> As mine is now, secession is but this.
> My kinsman's spirit calls me to assail
> The Fears that beat upon him for the Charter
> Which justifies your war and our defense,
> This Pythoness, whose oracles entail

Furious words and war! I shall not barter
Manhood for peace, though hating the offense
Which blots the page of reason with man's blood.
Your issue is not slavery, but to make
One vast republic, which will grow to be
Abroad a great aggressor, and at home
A despot, till a ruin overtake
The remnants of a shattered liberty.
The soul of Washington has been my guide,
The model of my action and my thought;
And he had fears your rule would override
The liberties of states and men. We ask
The Union as he made it, not as you
Would have it; and I bend me to the task
To break your yoke upon us, which has wrought
Destruction to our life and happiness;
And institute a government more true.
Your issue is not Slavery, but Gold,
And rulership of profits, to assess
Our toil by legal privilege, as of old.
You who applaud the Law of Laws were first
To strike it down, yet put us in the fault,
Who turn to revolution. At the worst
Slavery is injustice, will you halt
Injustice by a central tyranny?
If the slave suffer, will there never be
Suffering when you rule us in your rage?
The despot, the fanatic throw the gage
Of battle to us, and we take it up,
While your commander Grant keeps still the wage
Of bonded labor, and so fouls the cup

Whose handle shines: thus is it with your North.
But if injustice die not with this war,
And slavery die not, hopes of highest worth
Will die not. Revolution will abhor,
And battle Tyranny, as long as men
Plant by the sun, and by the constant star
Build temples to their hopes. And if we fail . . .

THE REPUBLIC

You hope not then to win?

LEE

                        They who are pale
Speak hopefully. They who still have hope
Speak words of half despair. But they who know
The future and hope not, are born to cope
With Destiny for God's sake, be the woe
And ruin what they will.

THE REPUBLIC

And you will lead,
And so misguide the flaming youth, the mad
And thoughtless spirits of young boys, unfreed
Of tutorship, the adventurous, who are glad
For tents and guns, and marches, and the thrill
Of battle, to their slaughter, and the ill
Of long catastrophe?

LEE

                  But they are read
In history which teaches hope, as I
Imbibed clear thoughts in youth. Their fathers bled

At Runnymede, at Concord, Valley Forge.
And they, the stock of eagles, winged and bred,
Will fly the heights, and flap the bloody gorge,
As their forefathers did.   They are so fleshed,
So spirited; and know that heated days
Dry up the roots of Liberty, which must,
Lest the whole tree from trunk to branch decays,
Be nourished into vigor and refreshed
By tyrants' blood and patriots' on the dust.
They have been taught rebellion: Milton's soul
Is on them, Locke's is on them, Washington's.
They need not my persuasion to enroll
Their spirits in this cause, who are the sons
Of spirits such as these!

THE REPUBLIC

So you resolve!
The Lord of Hosts, Jehovah, be upon you;
And trampled be the grapes of His wrath,
Seeing that my devotion has not won you
From the treason which my enemies revolve.
Be His disaster in your path,
And His security against the snake
Withdrawn to bruise your heel.   The Lord of Hosts
Has filled your hearts with evil dreams to walk
In vain imagination, till they break.
Thus says Jehovah: With wandering and wailing ghosts
I will fill your land, and make as powdered chalk
Your fruitfulness.   I will shut your cities up,
And shatter them as a potter's vessel;
And their foundations shall be broken as a cup,

Until My desolation shall possess all
Your cities amid the cities that are wasted.
The Lord of Hosts has sworn: As a wind of the wilderness
Scatters the stubble, henceforth do I scatter you,
Till Famine stink with death dews, which has tasted
My portion of bitter wormwood, washed with gall.
Be the children of the Southland fatherless;
And may the rags of ignominy tatter you;
And be your names the sport of a carnival
Of hissing, where all passers wag the head.
The Lord of Hosts has sworn: I will fill the South
With arm'd men as with caterpillars to devour you;
And I will choke with dust the treasonous mouth.
You shall be buried until the numerous dead
Shall have no burial, and wrath overpower you
Till you shall be as dung upon the ground.
You shall not be lamented.   And I will send
The lightning of my sword to wound,
Until you spue and fall and rise no more.
And you shall eat your sons, and the flesh of your friend,
In the days of the siege and the straitness,
When the shouts of triumphant righteousness walk before
The battle chariot of My greatness.
I will famish the toothless gums of pulers.
Your people shall labor in vain and in fire;
And I will break your captains and your rulers,
And drown your horses and riders in my ire.
Beasts shall devour you in the darkness of caves;
And pestilence shall enter at your forts;
Laughter shall sit upon your graves;
And I will rouse the Sea to starve your ports.

Your women shall be ravished, and your valleys
Of corn made desolate with flame;
And Lust and Rapine from your alleys
Shall fill your streets with Shame,
When I shall fling the torch among your cities,
And Charleston, Richmond and Atlanta burn,
Then you shall know I am the Lord who pities
No enemy until his spirit learn
Contrition and the worship of My word.
Thus I invoke Jehovah, the Lord
Of battles, Whom my North with fears,
And meditations worships, and whose Book
My North obeys, and faithfully reveres.
And in Jehovah's name I call and look
To Massachusetts and to Maine,
Vermont, Connecticut, New Hampshire and
My populous borders of the western plain;
And even I call Kentucky, Maryland,
And Tennessee to pour their strength and youth
From the fields and from the colleges in my hand:
The single-minded boys, who dream of truth,
The fearless, and the uncouth
Who think not, count not chances, but obey
Like hounds upon the hunt, and who will charge
When guns roar and baptismal blood is spilled,
And take my reasons, which they do not weigh,
But shout Jehovah's hymns along the marge
Of battle till my triumph be fulfilled.
Come then! I call! The Lord of Hosts has willed
My victory and the dawn of a better day!

LEE

I have resolved, and feel my soul sustained
By the God that you invoke that hate and force
Around my steps may be unchained.

(*He withdraws.*)

THE REPUBLIC

I call upon the Sea!

THE SEA

I will divorce
Their plenty, and their wharves shall rot.
I will watch as a dragon, and waylay
Their ships in every harbor, inlet, bay.
Your admonitions shall not be forgot!

THE REPUBLIC

I call upon the dead, the heroes of the past!

VOICES

Our favorable words shall tangle them, and be bent
By the heat of clamorous argument.
But these deserters shall be tied, made fast
By words of clearness favorable to you.

THE REPUBLIC

I call upon the rivers: the Father of Waters;
The great Ohio, which was made the line
Of freedom and of slavery.
I call upon the Tennessee,
The Cumberland to multiply the slaughters
Of my indomitable design!

THE RIVERS

After a season we shall free
Our ways for you, and with your ways combine.

THE REPUBLIC

I call upon the mountains, not to fall
And crush my enemies, but that they keep
No hiding places for the criminal
Foe when he flies for safety and for sleep;
And that they sentinel and watch the plains
When the rebels march against my capital;
And that they give me ores wherewith to break
Pharaoh's greed, and the murder which is Cain's;
And that they give me forges, which shall make
Shot, cannon, and the wheels of trains!

THE MOUNTAINS

Our stored up strength shall overtake
The Southern chivalry, as a coach is crushed
By an engine to the dust.
We will give you iron and coal,
Which shall enwrap Lee's armies and his soul,
And choke them as a serpent to submission.
All freedoms that delay or thwart your will,
Whether of press or speech shall be
Chained till your enemies shall feel contrition
For war, and in whatever peace shall come
We will enforce obedience to your word
By the down turning of our thumb,
Naked or gloved, that whatsoever be

Our strength shall be your strength, whether the sword
Or the scales of justice rule, till every knee
Shall bend before your laws, clothed with our might.
The South shall know the bog no longer yields
The steel wherewith victorious armies fight.
And they shall see triumphant battlefields
No more of charcoal, but of anthracite!

THE REPUBLIC

If it be so, I shall not fail.   Now smite
With your confederate strength, O, Sea;
And strike O, Mountains, and so be
The ruin and the overthrow of Lee!

> (*Arimanius and Ormund turn away.*)

ARIMANIUS

Would that Jehovah's Book and all His curses
Were in some fiery crater burned and lost.
In every war Hypocrisy rehearses
Their laws as on a day of Pentecost,
Which fired for ages Europe's bloody hell,
And Freedom slaughtered where they could not throttle.
What was the Fate that kept Ezekiel,
And lost for ages Plato, Aristotle?
Why treasured the seeds of ignorance and hate?
Why all the world's veins fouled with deadly poison?
Why coward railings that infuriate
These stronger arms, and waste the toiler's foison?

ORMUND

Yes, but the South as well would vindicate
Its vision by these very maledictions.

ARIMANIUS

Nothing so bad is as these moral fictions.
I'd throw the Hebrew Scriptures from the shelf.
I'd see the South make war for her convictions,
And fight not for Jehovah, but herself.

(*The scene closes.*)

ACT TWO

Scene: The battle field of Gettysburg.   Ormund and
     Arimanius on an eminence.   Night.

ARIMANIUS

Though Vicksburg's fallen, and the River taken,
Still if tomorrow Lee could but repeat
The skill of Fredericksburg—

ORMUND

                He is forsaken
By the genius which so long deferred defeat.

ARIMANIUS

I see his army wandering in retreat.
Veil we the future, and blot out the past!

ORMUND

All but Old Wooden Face will look aghast.

ARIMANIUS

See where he stands!   How silently he stalks!
How like a murderous idiot he gawks
Upon the tents!   Maggots crawling in gore
His vacant mouth fouls, and his fingers lean
Are forks with which he feeds himself gangrene.
Go by!   Be off!   Come to our eyes no more.

Fiend ridden Totem merciless and dense!
Why give him bugles, voices that adore?
Why give such reptile jaws omnipotence?
Such deafness music and such dumbness prayers?

ORMUND

He is the master in the world's affairs.

ARIMANIUS

He hears us not, or hearing little cares—
Look where he steals away!

ORMUND

          Close him from sight.
The stars are out.   How beautiful the night!

ARIMANIUS

How sweet these soldier boys are singing.   Hear!
The seaside voice, the prairie, pioneer.
Sweetly they mingle coming near and far.

ORMUND

Their fates will not when He has won the war.
                (*They walk over the field.*)

VOICES

John Brown's body lies a mouldering in the grave;
Old Missus marry—in the ranks of the Lord.
But John Brown's soul is marching with the brave—
When he put his arms around her—with his brave old
    sword,

Babylon is fallen—in de land ob cotton.
He is sworn as a private—dar am not forgotten.
Nicodemus the slave—in the ranks of the just.
Maryland, My Maryland—and moulder in the dust.

OTHER VOICES

Above the mists that feathered the pines, on the top of
    Lookout Mountain,
Among the nests where the eagles shrieked to the terrible
    cannonade;
Around the cliffs like a forest fire, as swift as a rising foun-
    tain,
The sons of the West climbed into the clouds, and never
    stopped or stayed.

The scarf of the fogs was stained with flame, the rocks ran
    blood, the thunder
And hail of the shot awoke the chasms from centuries of
    sleep,
As the sons of the South among the heights by lightning
    rent asunder
Battled the wrath of Hooker who fought his way along the
    steep.

Between Unaka and Chilowee the Cumberlands will
    remember;
And we looked down on the lower peaks, and the fruit of
    the battle knew;
The leaves of the clouds are blown in the blast of an era's
    mad September;
The heights appear, the land is green, for blood is dew.

OTHER VOICES

Consenting to desolation, we called their vision truth.
Be still their consecration the beauty of death in youth.

The peace of the grave be given us if their peace be vain;
And tyranny which has thriven, thrive over us again.

If Freedom bravely cherished passed to a reckless horde,
When the states as sovereigns perished with the loss of a
        freeman's sword;

And a spurious deed of warrant our freehold lands con-
        veyed,
Be all our work abhorrent as a lying trick of trade.

Upon the Ages' shoulders let Fate lay down the wrong
And Time show all beholders the Lust that fed the strong:

To summon force and plan it, and guide the iron heel
To crush such souls with granite, and break such hearts
        with steel.

VOICES OF THE MOUNTAINS

We are the Appalachians,
The walls of a great design,
Whose towers watch over the Nation's
Prairies of corn and wine.
Down from our sides the cold spring glides
To rivers that seaward flow
Through lowlands drawn by the ocean's tides,
Or west through the great plateau.

The hunter feet of Boone traversed
Our forests green and dark,
Before the dream of a continent burst
On the stardrawn path of Clark.
They sought the wilderness for land,
We stood becalmed with the dream
When anthracite should wake and stand
And rouse the giant steam.
We knew our strength would feed at length
The slender fingers of steel
That knit in the mills of the eastern hills
To the song of the loom and wheel.
The Ages manned our cavern shops,
And made our Titans toil,
Of steel and coal whose forehead drops
The bondage sweat of oil.
And even when the forges blazed
Which wrought the beam and truss
The slaves of Alabama raised
For strength no eyes to us.
And the masters raged who only saw
The crime of Brown, but we
Were welding wider chains of law
To slave before we free.

VOICES OF SOLDIERS

They battered us at Vicksburg,
They broke our cannon screens;
They shattered us at Donelson,
And captured New Orleans.
They seized our city Memphis,

And took our River too,
And then they marched through Tennessee,
And still the battle grew.
At Shiloh, at the landing
Of Pittsburg then we stood,
And tore at them and sabred them,
And made the river blood.
They huddled in a panic,
And hid among the wharves;
They cowered among the grasses where
We hunted them like dwarfs.
Then Grant came up and Buell,
And swung the gates of hell;
And still we stood and fought them
Till our commander fell.
In spite of steel and mountains,
And better shot and shell,
If Lee had only come along
When our commander fell,
The battle-field of Shiloh
Would have a tale to tell—
A different tale to tell.

The stars shine bright, and to-morrow is the battle;
And it's us for the word of Robert Lee.
But that deep sky reminds me of Stonewall Jackson—
And where may the soul of him be?

Way down the Shenandoah,
Sleeping in the cold, cold ground.
Stonewall Jackson, eagle, eagle!
Sleeping in the cold, cold ground!

Killed by the hunters he loved, and who loved him,
Hell's luck caught us again!
Stonewall Jackson leading in the thicket,
Beagle by the master slain.

Way down the Shenandoah
Sleeping in the cold, cold ground.
Stonewall Jackson, eagle, eagle,
Sleeping in the cold, cold ground!

Stonewall Jackson some of us will join you
Ere the smoke of this battle clear.
But I wouldn't have a doubt of to-morrow's battle,
If Stonewall Jackson were here.

Way down the Shenandoah,
Earth heals every wound.
But is that the victory, Stonewall Jackson,
Sleeping in the cold, cold ground?

Scene 2: Near Round Top on the battle-field of Gettys-
　　　burg.　Night.　Ormund and Arimanius.

ORMUND

You do not like this chosen battle-field?

ARIMANIUS

It is the accident of an accident.
I wish the causing cause could be repealed.
Lee did not dream the Gettysburg event
When his poor soldiers hither came for shoes.

Lee did not order battle nor intend
First guns to fire here. Now the fate accrues
And must continue to the tragic end.

ORMUND

First need of shoes and then the cannon roar!

ARIMANIUS

His irony is farcical as of yore—
Look! Wooden Face again—

ORMUND

He frightens you.

ARIMANIUS

I'm sorry for these boys. Look where he goes
To Cemetery Ridge!

ORMUND

Let's see it too.

ARIMANIUS

I would to Lee's tent whom the hours oppose.

Scene 3: Before Lee's tent. Longstreet and an officer.

OFFICER

I never knew Lee in such restlessness
As he is now; he cannot sleep to-night.
Danger is used to tense his iron nerves.
At Chancellorsville amid the raining bullets

Calmly he stood in talk of books and schools.
And once I saw him under fire stoop down
To pick a wounded sparrow from the ground.
But now he walks, or sits with knitted brows,
Or clasps his hands, which he unclasps again,
And looks and glows.

LONGSTREET

      That's his audacity
That paces, crouches, and surveys the leap;
When he uncloaks his caution, have no fear
That his audacity will fail him, for
This swift invasion of the North is such,
And his command to storm their lines to-morrow.
This he had done before except for me,
Who by dissent and argument have stayed
The ruin of that course. He'd hazard all,
And fears not—yet for thinking cannot sleep.
Go to your rest. I'll see him once again,
Once more I'll reason with him.

    (The officer leaves. Longstreet enters Lee's tent.)

LEE

I am resolved. At dawn the grand assault.
Send every soldier of our army up
The Ridge and take it, nothing spare. You see
How gallantly we've held the Federals
With half their force. So order up my boys,
Who go where they are told, take any chance,
Hungry and shoeless as they are.

LONGSTREET

                    I know.
And that's the pity.   You have never met
Defeat, no Waterloo, and that you may not
I plead with you against this.

LEE

                    It must be.
In taking counsel I have paused too long;
And what I ordered did not come to pass:
Stuart who came not and who went astray;
Hill who commenced this battle without order;
Ewell who failed to seize the golden chance
Of the first day when we were victors all
But capturing the Hill, their general killed,
Their forces in retreat.   Then one brigade
Of these, my boys, in spite of all defaults
Of Stuart, Hill, had brought us victory.
It is too bad, but not too late to win,
Not if we strike, and strike at break of dawn,
With every man strike.   Strike with every gun.
Strike with the men of Pickett.   So attend
This my command and strike.

LONGSTREET

                    It shall be so.
I shudder, but obey.

   (*Ormund and Arimanius turn away and walk the battle-
      field.*)

VOICES

He has gone to be a soldier in the army of the Lord;
He is sworn as a private in the ranks of the Lord;
He shall stand at Armageddon with his brave old sword,
  When heaven is marching on.

ARIMANIUS

As if the powers of good and evil were
Contending here on God's great battle day.
Men would be gods and clothe a massacre
With meaning which shall never pass away.

ORMUND

That Voice! It is this field's interpreter:
Government of the people still must be,
Nor ever fail, nor perish from the earth.

ARIMANIUS

That Voice! Which condescends with charity,
Denying malice, when he saw its birth
Fed with these slaughters after sorcery
Had robbed the truth of power the sword to stay.
What giant self-crowned apotheosis
That pleads its firmness in the right to slay,
As if God had revealed Himself in his
Vision of truth which none shall disobey.
That Voice! Which says if every drop of blood
Drawn by the lash the sword a drop shall pay,
And that the bondsman's stolen wealth be sunk
Still that the judgments of the Lord are good—

How good the Lord is when we have our way!
What wine of furious vengeance has he drunk
Who thus protests the hate his words betray?
That Voice! With all these specious reasons fudging
Till Truth has nothing of the Lie begrudged.
That Voice! Which having judged forbids a judging,
And having slain sees righteousness adjudged.

ORMUND

Why let your soul by passing things be shaken?

ARIMANIUS

I hate to see the spoil of battle taken
As foragers who gather up refuse
After the feast when noble diners rise
For great events of memory and the Muse.

ORMUND

Look! how the silvers of the dawn suffuse
The paling posterns of the western skies.
The sun now like a lantern under water
Spreads starry light, and hues of lavender
From richer lanterns light the visible wall
Of heaven.

ARIMANIUS

            Now the camps begin to stir.
Soon now His sword will sate itself on slaughter.
Now fires and talk! I hear the bugles call!

ORMUND

Disaster now that Time shall not retrieve.
Lee limps henceforward to the trap of Grant.

ARIMANIUS

I hear the croaking of the cormorant.
Come! To an eminence to watch and grieve.

Scene 4: The battle-field.   Afternoon.   Lee and Longstreet; afterwards Pickett.

LEE

The day wanes. What's the matter? Tell me why
This long delay?

LONGSTREET

My reasons I renew
Against your plan.

LEE

No! No! At once attack.
Put the whole corps in action. Summon Hood,
McLaws, Heth, Pickett, Bender, summon Hill.
With every man, gun, gunner, horseman strike.
Strike at their center, take the ridge.

LONGSTREET

'Tis done.
(*Lee goes away.   Pickett enters.*)

PICKETT

When do we start?

LONGSTREET

Now! What's your strength?

PICKETT

Twelve thousand.

LONGSTREET

Bring up your Carolinians and Virginians,
Lead the assault. Strike at the Federal center.

PICKETT

I'll take it sir.

LONGSTREET

I hope so. God be with you.

Scene 5: An eminence. Ormund and Arimanius. Arimanius to himself:

From the groves, from the thickets, over fields, through
    hollows,
From the sun-scorched ridges where the air steams blood;
Ranks broken, ranks reformed where the spent ball wal-
    lows,
On to battle strides Virginia in the red run mud.
Forward march! thunders Pickett with a sun smitten
    sword,
You are lean young victors who have never known defeat.

Hit the line! Pierce the center! Take the Hill is the word.
Crush the despot, the abhorred! Track the enemy's
    retreat!—
Lee has ordered. Up! Forward! Drums beat!

They are youths high born. They are lettered hearts and
    wise.
They are gentlemen and heroes, as they fight, as they
    fought.
Their knapsacks were their pillows, and their tents were
    the skies.
And they ate the flour and bacon as they watched, as they
    wrought.

What is hunger, what is thirst, what is rain, heat, cold?
For they make their body's pangs just a triumph for the
    soul.
How they swing round the rocks with the smoke of battle
    rolled
On their shattered ranks replenished as they file up the
    knoll!

And the canisters waylay them, but nothing can dismay
    them,
And but a trice delay them, as they mount to close range;
Cross fields strong fenced, as the cannoneers essay them—
And where is their artillery that it makes no exchange?

Where are the other troops to sustain, and fight through?
Where is Davis? Where's Archer? Where's Wilcox?
    Where is Scales?

Where the seasoned men of yesterday who followed
    Pettigrew?
Look! Pickett leads alone! Look the grand assault fails!

And the Federals in their trenches wait and watch, watch
    and wait
For the blood that fury quenches. And revenge each
    captain clenches
For the shame of Fredericksburg. So they steady down
    their hate
Till their victims clad in gray are two hundred yards
    away—
Oh, such breasts to tear with shot, but such hearts to
    take the Hill.—
Now they open up the canisters, chain-shot, musket shot,
Gap the ranks which stop not, but shout, climb, will.
The three brigades of Pickett in double time and drill
Assault the trenches' center spot, and face the fiery grill,
And flap their tattered banners where the flying bullets
    shrill.
They shriek now, they leap now, they fall now, they surge;
They stagger now, advance now, the line is almost made.
Look! Garnett drops dead now leading his brigade!
See round him they close in now, fill up now, converge.
They leap the outer works now, and with the foeman
    merge.
Now hand to hand, now bayonets, and now the bloody
    mire.
The howling mass is writhing, and grapples and embraces.
Who is friend, who is foe, who dares to fire?
Arms fall, breasts gush, butts mash faces.

But they have pierced the center, they enter and re-enter;
But they have pierced the center, the Federals fall back;
Now an instant's silence and then the rifles' crack
Around the mad Virginian renewing the attack.
Then Cushing from a clump of trees flings the wild canister;
Again the Hill is black, down the slope a wrack
Of Pickett's men are drifting like a misty blur;
Now comes Armistead, already half bled,
Hat upon his sword perched the battery to seize.
There Cushing waits him behind a grove of trees,
There mans the cannon which the grape shot frees,
There makes the thunder on the great tube keys—
There they fall together in the grove of trees.

It is finished. They have died. They have failed!
    They have failed!

ORMUND

They have lost the cause, the heights, if the heights are
    merely earth.

ARIMANIUS

Thus their great belief was vanquished, if their great
    belief availed
Not for them the proud flight, not for us the new birth.

ORMUND

What's the battle's end for them, changed to nature in a
    breath?
Living not to prop hope, pray for faith, crawl to springs.
Merging souls so rapt with Time—is it life, is it death?
Dying so can there be veering to the passion of their
    wings?

ARIMANIUS

Grief for him who knows the issue, walks away lest he see
How they come not back who pressed where he pointed
    them to go.
Arms around his horse's neck, eyes averted, lingers Lee,
Taking all the fault for his, and the burden of the woe.

ORMUND

That Voice again! What music out of pain;
What sweet west wind blown from the western plain:—
These dead who died here did not die in vain.
From their heroic sacrifice a birth
Must come of larger love and liberty;
And government of the people still must be,
Nor ever fail nor perish from the earth.
Freedom embattled here was loved of both
The North and South who fought to keep her troth;
So Freedom shall renew her ancient worth,
For thus is registered the people's oath.

Scene 6: Lee's Headquarters at Gettysburg. Lee and
                Pickett.

PICKETT

We have returned.   We stormed and took the Ridge.
We took it who climbed to it—and we died.
We took it, then we died and lost the prize.
We kept it for a moment, then we died.
We fought alone unaided; we obeyed.

LEE

The fault is mine.   What of my gunner Pelham?
My boy, my eagle with his feathers blown
By lightning and by thunder?   Where's that face
Of starry wonder?

PICKETT

By his cannon's wheel.

LEE

Triumph is for the buglers of the hour,
And after that may pass with those who won it.
But valor in defeat is Beauty's brother,
And Truth's and Love's, sons of Eternal Law.
Pickett my reverence.   These are the souls
Whom death defeats not.   Though the purple rocks,
Which shore Death's soundless island, crush their craft,
They leap and sink not with the shattered prows
Of circumstance, but climb the crags of Fate,
Escape the sinking hulks of life and climb,
And reach the heights that know no setting sun
Until the world's sun set.   So for their faith
We stand here and await the enemy.
If he attack us not then we retire.

PICKETT

We will obey.

LEE

Go to your sleep now.

PICKETT

What is sleep to me?

Scene 7: Near Lee's Tent.   Night.   Ormund and
                    Arimanius.

VOICES

John Brown's body lies a mouldering in the grave;
John Brown's body lies a mouldering in the grave;
John Brown's body lies a mouldering in the grave;
          His soul goes marching on.

John Brown's body was hung to a tree;
John Brown died that a people might be free;
John Brown's soul has conquered Captain Lee,
          His soul is marching on.

              Glory, glory hallelujah,
              Glory, glory hallelujah,
              His soul is marching on.

ARIMANIUS

Look at that phantom figure whose regard
Is on Lee's tent door as if keeping guard
That Lee escape not.   And around him stand
Ghosts of his followers, a lawless band.
Surely a bigot's faith is hard to stifle.

ORMUND

One hand of him is gripped around a rifle;
He holds the Bible in the other hand.

ARIMANIUS

Yes, he of grizzled beard and granite frown—
It is no other surely than John Brown,

Whom Lee at Harper's Ferry took, and now
His ghost returns to execute the vow. . . .
What is my use in all this retrograde
Fate of the world, which folly overruns?
Would I might see its destiny remade
Divorced from superstition and from guns,
The instruments of minds that pray and kill. . . .
What is my use?   I am a wasted spirit;
Time and this battle run against my will;
My soul's a wanderer, and no truths ensphere it.

ORMUND

You must submit.   There is no good or ill;
But all is good or ill for your perceiving.
Fate is so long it's told in nonpareil;
To know the threads may be your heart's deceiving
About the pattern that the loom is weaving.

ARIMANIUS

Let us away to spaces high and clear;
Let us seek out some peasant, mountaineer.
Soon will the war end.   But we now behold
The might of steel, the sorcery of gold.
John Brown's rebellion at the last financed
By the New Commerce looks with fat disdain
On genius and its hope discountenanced
By factories and steel and fields of grain.
And Lee entangled in the wilderness
Outnumbered will in failure acquiesce.

ORMUND

His failure shall enlarge man's life and bless
Through Duty which shall lead him and uphold.
Men from a palsied bed no less may sway
A family, tenantry with judgment, faith;
The sword falls and the mind upon its way
Leaves and ascends to space of sweeter breath.
Defeated on one plane is to be freed
To higher levels, where if one succeed
Means purer blossoms and a rarer seed.

ARIMANIUS

Such rising is withdrawal, for the law
Of freedom is to give the soul its own.

ORMUND

The soul to have its freedom must withdraw.

ARIMANIUS

And to be free the soul must be alone.

ORMUND

Faith with one's self upon the will imposes
Withdrawal from the wills whose touch distracts;
And so the world whose creed is counting noses
Drives into exile those who spurn its pacts.

ARIMANIUS

Let us away to pines and cataracts,
The Future better there its work discloses.

(The scene ends.)

ACT THREE

A mountain side of the Alleghanies before the door of a log cabin, the home of a mountaineer. It is early morning. First Ormund and Arimanius. Then a deserter from Lee's army appears. He is bare footed, ragged and hungry.

ARIMANIUS

These swirling mists below us fade and melt
Like Pickett's men down Cemetery Hill.

ORMUND

Look! How the heaven like a vernal veldt
Heals as it smiles on every transient ill.
Earth took them to its heart which reconciles
All fate which like the sunlight broods and smiles.

ARIMANIUS

A youth approaches. Let us loiter near
Better to see his face, better to hear
What's said between him and this mountaineer.

ORMUND

Deserting he approaches full of fear.

MOUNTAINEER

Who are you stranger?

SOLDIER

A traveler.

MOUNTAINEER

And where bound?

SOLDIER

To find my wife and children.

MOUNTAINEER

Where are they?

SOLDIER

Some place in West Virginia.

MOUNTAINEER

You don't know?

Lost in the war perhaps.

SOLDIER

Yes, lost in the war.

MOUNTAINEER

While you were in the army?

SOLDIER

In the army.

MOUNTAINEER

Don't be afraid.   I know you.   For the dust
And gray of your gray uniform reveal
Your southern character.

SOLDIER

                    I am starved and worn,
And sick, so be my friend.

MOUNTAINEER

                    Of course your friend!
Here's water, and here's food.

SOLDIER

                    Your southern blood
Shows southern hospitality.

MOUNTAINEER

                    Yes, southern blood,
But for the Union; born in Tennessee,
A distant kinsman of the hunter Boone,
Who crossed these mountains in an early day.
Too old to fight, but friendly to the Union,
As many were in Tennessee, up here
Among these mountains, pines, and eagles, clouds,
Where I have lived these twenty years, and reared
Six sons who went to battle for the Union.
One killed at Shiloh, one at Chickamaugua,
And one at Antietam. . . .

SOLDIER

                    I was there.

MOUNTAINEER

And fought against my son, or killed him, maybe?

SOLDIER

I pray to God it be not so!

MOUNTAINEER

You pray?

SOLDIER

I pray.   And none can understand our army
Who does not know our army prayed, and all
Its leaders prayed, our Jackson and our Lee.

MOUNTAINEER

Here in the mountains we forget to pray.
The Almighty seems too near for us to pray;
But we believe because the mountains make us,
And love our friends, and try to live as men.
Here take my hand, boy, for you are my kinsman.

SOLDIER

Your kinsman?

MOUNTAINEER

Yes, we are Americans!
These are our mountains, yours and mine, my boy.
Yonder is our Virginia, never lost,
Though bent on straying from the Union's fold.

And yonder in the west is our Ohio,
Which never strayed . . . and all this land is ours
This vast America.   And do you know
What saved it, or will save it?

SOLDIER

No!

MOUNTAINEER

These mountains!

Rest now a little, take your food, and later
I'll tell you about America, and these mountains,
Where since the war I've lived and all alone.
My woman died with heartbreak when that son
Was killed at Antietam.

SOLDIER

Oh, too bad!

MOUNTAINEER

Yes, and I dug her grave beside that pine tree,
And buried her one day in falling rain.
Next day the sun shone, and the birds were singing,
And all the pine trees dirged her, and a peace
Entered my heart for thinking of her wonder,
Who bore these sons and loved me to the end.

SOLDIER

Oh, I am happy to be here with you.
Let me abide a little and get rested.

MOUNTAINEER

Long as you want, my boy. The fare is plain:
Wild game and hominy, and mountain dew—

SOLDIER

I never drink.

MOUNTAINEER

Well, if you need a soother.
But how's the war?

SOLDIER

The South is all but conquered.

MOUNTAINEER

It had to come. I knew it from the first.

SOLDIER

How so?

MOUNTAINEER

These mountains told me. By and by
I'll tell you what I mean about these mountains,
Learned from my labors when I helped to bore
Their walls with tunnels, and to loop their gorges
With iron rails, while all your Southland dreamed.
And so the South is all but whipped?—thank God!
You started boy—forgive me. . . .

SOLDIER

It is nothing.
I shall endure such words while life endures.
My fate, you know.

MOUNTAINEER
What book is that you have?

SOLDIER
Thucydides.

MOUNTAINEER
What is this language?

SOLDIER
Greek!

MOUNTAINEER
And you read Greek?

SOLDIER
I read it.

MOUNTAINEER
You're a scholar.
Who are you boy?

SOLDIER
A deserter from Lee's army!

MOUNTAINEER
Oh, but I mean what were you at the first?

SOLDIER
What matter's that, since I have turned deserter?

MOUNTAINEER
Why grieve so for a thing you chose to do?

SOLDIER

Our soldier hearts were breaking by the thousand,
For we were hunted in the Wilderness;
And we were shoeless, ragged, we were hungry;
And we were sleepless, sick, and we were dying;
And we were doomed to conquest, and we saw it.
And all the while our wives and mothers wailed,
And wrote us to come home, for they were starving,
And needed us to earn their bread again.
What could we do but die for a lost cause?
But there are some who stick, O, valiant hearts!
While thousands have deserted, even myself,
Who could no more endure the tear-soaked letters
My little wife was writing . . . God forgive me,
Or seal the eyes of memory lest they see
The sovran eagle whom the eagles left
To beat his dauntless wings among the thickets!
O, Lee, my general, my hunted eagle,
O, gentle, just, forgiving, fearless—victor
If half supported, still I see your face,
As last I saw it, when you rode among us
With words of comfort, praise, encouragement—
And I deserted you, O pale, great face!
Deserted you, O gray, but dauntless hair!
Would I had fallen, not your son in battle,
Fallen at Antietam, not your son!

MOUNTAINEER

But if you pray, boy, you believe all's well.
If never a soldier had deserted, Lee
Would lose the battle. Would you know the cause?

SOLDIER

We were outnumbered . . .

MOUNTAINEER

Yes, but see these mountains!
Now tell me of yourself, and of the war.

SOLDIER

Well, but these mountains, which you chant, relate
How they are critical.

MOUNTAINEER

Oh, I will tell you.
But first how goes the war? These many months
No letters from my sons, and in this loft
Remote I hear but little, and these weeks
No word at all.

SOLDIER

Have you not heard of Lee?
How Grant is wearing down the strength of Lee?
How Lee depletes the ranks of Grant, which fill
As fast as they are thinned?

MOUNTAINEER

Which Lee were wise,
The South too, and yourself, to have foreseen.

SOLDIER

We didn't, and no matter if we had:
We saw a vision, and we had a faith.

MOUNTAINEER

What faith?

SOLDIER

The faith they taught my soldier father
At West Point!

MOUNTAINEER

What was that?

SOLDIER

Secession's right,
Taught North as well as South before the war;
Believed in North and South for sixty years,
And now untaught in blood.

MOUNTAINEER

You are not changed!

SOLDIER

Look! I have read. Look at these handled pages!

MOUNTAINEER

What is the argument?

SOLDIER

That the South's submission
Was slavery.

MOUNTAINEER

That written there in Greek?

SOLDIER

The world is old, and all its faiths are old.
The North is Sparta, and Athens is the South;
The North is victor, Sparta was the victor,
And Athens' light went out, as now the gleams
Of Liberty are dying where the Wilderness
Tangles the feet of Lee, our Pericles.
And those who fell at Gettysburg should have
Lee, but not Lincoln for their intercessor.

MOUNTAINEER

All strange to me!   And stranger still the word
That you believed this book, and therefore fought.

SOLDIER

Oh, I was one of thousands whose intent,
And hearts were so instructed.   That's your fault
Not to know this, and therefore not to know
Our spirit.   For your soldiers left the fields;
But we rushed from the campus, and the class-room;
And our slaves, loyal to us—commentary
Upon your slanders of our mastership!—
Labored in gladness to produce the food
That fed our soldiers.   There were thousands of us,
Who closed the calculus, our Pindars, Homers,
To fly against your Sparta; and I left
Sweet dreams and studies there at Charlottesville,
And sweeter things than they, a wife and child,
And a child to be, to battle for my faith,
And follow Lee—

MOUNTAINEER

Whom you forsook at last?

SOLDIER

Because the war was hopeless, and my mind
Broke with the grief for failure, and these cries
Of mouths that starved; and incoherent thought,
And will that could not order and array
Clear reasons, and compact them to a course,
The fruit of terror, hunger and despair.
So my judgment fell, till in a sudden mood,
I fled, and having started madly, ran
Until return was bad as going on. . . .

I am better now, but there are days enough
Between the Wilderness and this mountain side,
Of which my memory is a mist, which thins
To vacancy, as even now that cloud
Fades and reveals the inane above the peak.
So what I did must answer for my faith.
Who will forget us, nor in Time's remembrance
Include not me among that ragged band?
Us the ill-shod, the hungry, without arms?
Us who with Bibles, and with books of Greek
Kept heart, and sang and fought? Us trim and young,
White limbed, with dancing eyes and glistening teeth,
Eager to live and act out hero words
Written in ancient stories, and to die
As died Athenians, and O, blissful vision,
To be sweet names forever, like deathless airs

That stir around a sunny promontory
From fragrant islands, breathing the sound of words
As musical as harps.   O, mountaineer,
You handed roughly as an eagle's claw,
And eyed to pierce the distance over valleys,
And up these misty slopes, we were a breed
Never to be despised, for we were brave
Gentlemen to the core, who followed Lee,
And by his deathless genius swept your North
From the very gates of Richmond, and won the field
Of Chancellorsville, where fate, too hard to bear,
The twin of Lee, the terrible eagle fell,
Our Jackson—what disaster!

MOUNTAINEER

Sent of God!

SOLDIER

It must be.   For with Jackson we had won
The war, now lost, and which could not be lost
Save God so wills it, as he willed between
An Antietam, where we held them back,
We unprovisioned, and half armed, against
The fresh, the armed, the numerous.   So along
These desperate years we followed and obeyed
Our Lee, and saw him crush them one by one,
The Northern captains sent to conquer him:
Pope, Hooker and McClellan routed all,
Or stayed, their armies rolled up like a scroll
And hurled beyond dividing rivers.   Glorious
And dreadful war!

MOUNTAINEER

But there was Gettysburg!

SOLDIER

And there was Jackson's death before that day;
And there was Stuart's cavalry, which failed;
And there was Longstreet, who delayed; and we
Some sixty thousand weaker than the North
Entrenched upon the heights, and fenced about
With cannon thick as cactus—which we stormed!
I was among that fated force, which swarmed
Through orchards, meadows, over fences, flew
The fiery ridge, and took it amid the hail
Of bullets, and the meteors of the cannons;
And thought that we had triumphed, till I saw
That we had made the dread assault alone
Against a foe ten times as great as ours,
Protected by the rocks, and which from trenches
Slaughtered us as we climbed.   There sorely wounded
I limped to shelter; and never from that day
Have been what once I was in body or mind . . .
Which gives me no excuse for being here.
Sweet is it to hope, but sweet to hope no more,
When what we thought was land, and made us strive
In pain to reach its drifting shores, takes wing
As fog and fades, while all the sky and sea
Are clear beneath an unclouded sun. So now
All sorrows begin to lift: and if I sink
In a life too vast, and with the South I loved
Perish, 'tis better than to wake and trim
Sails that the mocking destiny out-flies.

MOUNTAINEER

Calamity has brought you to the truth.
Now you must see your feet on solid earth,
And tread the soil of a new America!

SOLDIER

How can it be? What time can heal the wounds,
The ravages you made, who fought to win,
Regarding not the means? While we made war
As gentlemen, obeying Lee.

MOUNTAINEER

                    All means
Are right to put rebellion down.

SOLDIER

                         Even so
You acted in your wrath. So Sheridan
Ripped Shenandoah, nor left a living thing.
And so your Sherman cut our South in two,
And ruined, burned and slaughtered. So your fleet
Sealed up our ports; and so our children starve,
Whose cries unnerve us, as I am unnerved,
And so deserted. And so the crimes of war
Always reviled when peace is, and men read,
Have been repeated amid the shouts and thanks
Of you, who pray. . . . It was not so with Lee,
Who did not spoil, or ply the torch, but warred
As a knight would war, and bought what he had seized
By force, if he had willed it. God! who knows

The truth of all this welter?   Give me faith
To see my general victor in the realm
Of Thought, and though in strength below the brute,
Was in his god-like bearing more than man
In Truth's defeat, and a victor whom no foe
Can overcome with less nobility.

MOUNTAINEER

What of him in the Wilderness to-day?

SOLDIER

A captive, or a prize of death, who knows?
Richmond had fallen before I fled.   But when
Lee started on retreat, with Petersburg
Stormed and reduced, and our huddled few were caught
In a crescent of fire, with Sheridan, Sherman, Grant
To clasp it tighter; and they captured us
Ten thousand strong, then what were best to do,
Fly, or be captured, since we were denied
Battle and death in battle under Lee?

MOUNTAINEER

All's well, my boy.   Since Vicksburg fell to Grant,
And the River flowed for us, and not for you;
And since the Sea assailed you; since you lost
Rather by thought than arms, the border lands,
And this Virginia of the West, beyond
These mountains, what could be, but what has come?
Now you are on your way—

SOLDIER

                    Direct me, friend.

MOUNTAINEER

Come! We ascend!

                         Now look! These are the hills
Which have undone you, as they made the North
Strong while subduing them to use, while you
Remained an easy people, slipping through
The natural gates of water to the Gulf
With cotton, growing soft and fat thereby.
For since these granite walls did not oppose
Your dreams of empire, so you slept and dreamed,
And weakened in your riches, softly gained.
But we, the North, the Northwest, bound to hack,
And blast and dig for turnpikes and canals,
Grew mighty with our labors.   And scarce were done
These ways of commerce, when the wonder wheels
Of steam began to race these rocky heights,
And shout along these cuts, and join with trade
The populous East, and the toiling, fertile West.
And what were Greek and prayers against the rails
That re-surveyed old sections and their hates,
And made the North and Northwest, and the East,
And even your South, against its will, at one?
The underground was but a little thing,
And teased you only . . . but these rails of steel
Subdued you while you slept; and you will come
Not free of them, until your South is new,
And by acceptance of their rulership,
Become their ruler and their tributary.
Slaves fed your soldiers, but the reaper fed
Our soldiers, and more richly than your slaves . . .
I am not lettered, but the arm that toils

Makes thought more clear, and the eye more sure
To see and weigh.   Virginia and the slope
Of all that East, where Lee by battle skill
Has stayed the overflowing of the West,
Were but the limbs, and are the limbs that fall,
Or live, as falls or lives the tree, whose growth
Is rooted in the Valley of the West.
And as it lived by Grant, so shall Virginia
Live newly, as a limb released from ropes
Which could not drag the tree, tugged by the arm
Time shriveled, age discarded.   And what matter
Whether your Lee fought on, surrendered, fell?
And matters nothing your desertion.   Son
Your prayers were not to God, but to a god
Dead as the fish god, which in helplessness
Saw Samson wreck the Temple!   But these mountains
Are better churches, built for surer prayers . . .
To them you should have prayed! See yonder now,
Here from these heights, the land of corn, the vast
Prairies of the West, far to the River
Ruled by the Corn, and by that rulership
Ruling the land, the South that was, and is
To be, the East that is and will be.

SOLDIER
Corn!
Crops, riches! Let them fall in earth and die,
Else do they bide alone, and naught produce
But riches, crops.   By these are we undone.
The ancient goddess of the corn was served
By sacrifice that has not passed away—
Pigs smoked upon her altar.

MOUNTAINEER

That's a waste,
The thrifty custom was to burn a goat.

SOLDIER

Not to this goddess of the underworld,
Whom heaven favors—that's her peril too.
Some one is coming! Listen! There he is!
A horseman hasting.

MOUNTAINEER
Just a traveler.

HORSEMAN

Hooray!

ECHOES

Hooray! Hooray!

MOUNTAINEER
Hooray for what?

ECHOES

For what?

HORSEMAN

Lee has surrendered!

ECHOES

Surrendered! Surrendered!

HORSEMAN

Send the word along!

ECHOES

Along! Along!

HORSEMAN

At Appomattox!

ECHOES

Appomattox! Appomattox!

HORSEMAN

War's over!

ECHOES

Over, over, over! e-e-r-r-r!

(The horseman disappears singing.)

HORSEMAN

John Brown's body lies a mouldering in the grave,
    His soul is marching on.

ECHOES

His soul is marching on—on—on—on—on!

ARIMANIUS

On, but no farther than the pulpit spouters
Who fled to Europe when the scamp was hung.

ORMUND

Even the echoes ratify the word
Of Destiny, and all the mountains heard.

ARIMANIUS

Government of the people cannot be
Save Brown's soul walk behind the soul of Lee.
John Brown is hate, and never Liberty
Lives where a people act and live in hate.
Hate is the principle of tyrannies.
Good will enlightens; only tolerance frees.
Let us to Powhatan.

ORMUND

Just as you please.

(*They pass out. Meanwhile the mountaineer stands,
watching the soldier who is bowed in tears.*)

MOUNTAINEER

Come, come, my boy, leave off these foolish tears.
Soon will you see your children and your wife.
Look, you are young! Build with the country. Lift
Your heart up to the new day. Hear the corn
Already greening all the West, the pines
That catch its song. Go now, and peace be yours.
There lies your way.

SOLDIER

If only I can forget
What lies behind these mountains whence I came.
I must forget it. Mountaineer farewell.

MOUNTAINEER

Farewell.

(*The soldier descends to the western valley. The mountaineer with shaded eyes watches him as long as he can
be seen; then turns and ascends the mountain. The
scene closes.*)

Scene 2: Ormund and Arimanius on one of the hills over-
        looking Richmond.

ARIMANIUS

That island yonder gathering stick and floss
Is where John Smith his Pocahontas leaving
Sailed up from Jamestown here to plant the cross.

ORMUND

Much was it past his fancy or believing
What Fate upon this landscape would engross.

ARIMANIUS

If it was Belle Isle where he set it up,
His blind hand followed some symbolic vision:
There maggot food, and there the putrid cup
Were served to skeletons in Libby Prison.
Hatred the soil of hatred ever fallows,
The prison keeper will adorn the gallows.
When will the soil grow sterile, nor produce?

ORMUND

The answer to your question is abstruse.
Revenge once vanished in Apollo's grove.

ARIMANIUS

You mean enlightenment, but scarcely love?

ORMUND

The first is where the second soon will be.
The second well conduces to the first.

ARIMANIUS

Flame blackened City! How with poverty,
And sick humiliation are you cursed.
No stone upon another would have rested
If Lincoln walking through you had been killed.
In his own capital, as if heaven jested,
His blood upon the angry earth was spilled.
Yet had it been beside the ancient shrine
Where Patrick Henry with heroic breath
Aroused Virginia with his leonine
Alternative of Liberty or Death;
Or by this mansion of the dominant judge
Whose surface reasoning was alone impartial;
For Lincoln's eloquence betrays the trudge
And logic phalanx of Chief Justice Marshall—
So had his western blood confirmed the oath
Of Henry, or the judge's logic twisting.

ORMUND

The future of the country runs with both.
The hill makes stronger by the hill's resisting.

ARIMANIUS

I had not willed it so. Now is inflamed
The furious North, almost with rabies blind.
For this great sorrow how can Lee be blamed,
Save from a mad and truth-deserted mind?
Both Lincoln, Lee but did the work before them.

ORMUND

There have you now the secret, and the whole
Fate, work and problem of the human soul.
Crises and wars, however you deplore them,
However you approve them, have control.
Whether you shirk the battle or fight through
You spurn the false or else accept the true—
And they are naught save what they are to you.
With Him the rest is, and He only knows
What the end is, and what the world should do.

ARIMANIUS

Nothing so sad is as a man in sleep,
A child, a woman, nothing sadder is.
I wonder if He will remembrance keep
Of all His dead ones at the armistice?
When on the earth the Kingdom of Heaven comes
Will He remember all his millions sleeping,
Who fought and died for fair milleniums,
Who sowed but died before the day of reaping?
Will He with pity view them? What remembrance
If in the Kingdom they are not to share,
These faithful ones who led the great advance,
Whose flaming spirits never knew despair?
Lincoln is dead, Lee soon himself departs,
These leaders are they better fortuned than
The privates who believed in them with hearts
That asked not but obeyed the master plan?
If Lee nor Lincoln see the Kingdom, or
Know it has come as little as these hills
This contest is a drove of ants at war—

ORMUND

How do you know the destiny He wills?
Since every growth is to some living end,
Are thought, desire, love: seeds of this hour
To lie unblossomed and self-sepulchered?
Seeds that are made as seeds, but have no friend
In wings or winds, uncarried and unshed;
Gifted to sense new triumphs and transcend
Sleep in the shell which stirs, with hopes sustained
As the seed is; with restlessness to break
The prison of the present, and remake
Life, yet to lie unfruitful and restrained?
The hand that builds the rocks, the earthen mass
Stops with a world of mountains, seas and streams;
Another Hand in correspondence takes
The toil of life through living things that pass
From hunger and from mating to the dreams
Of man who sees, as consciousness awakes,
Oneness and difference, and the soul which makes
Relationship and unison again,
Created but traced over on the plane
Of conscious thought, the final consummation.
And thus the great ascent, the great vocation
Of life is but an endless imitation,
And ever to itself is a returning.
Thought once achieved, the Genius of creation
Put by the finished body for the learning
Of what the soul's deep uses are and powers,
Crowned now with will to rule the earth, select
Survivals once determined by the blind
Hand of the demi-gorgon, now by mind.

Do we not see the root itself which flowers
In beasts and men, upon the disparate sprays
Of instinct and of mind, and mind which strays
And branches to the blossom of the soul?
For that which moves the cells to break, depart
And find their place and make at last a heart,
Or gather here and make a voice an eye
Works with these instruments to verify,
Search out more life, find truth more deep.
Eyes come from practiced thought which works in sleep;
And vision by long æons of desire
Will come to man, now sensing a life of light
Beyond, above this age of smouldering fire.
The will which spurned the earth, became a tree,
Shed crawling scales, and blossomed wings that fly,
Escaped the shell of instinct to be free
As thought, did not exhaust the mounting power
Which puts new tendrils forth of aspiration.
Its breath will bring the wingéd visitation
Which shall impregnate life to larger flower.
The city crowned, republic rule of man
Comes last served by the Genius which sustains
The individual and the race to be.
And after that the vision of other goals
Than life on earth in a universe of souls.

ARIMANIUS

After the life dance as the summer wanes,
As nature, if not symbol, prophecy
The oft repeated play of earth we see:
The well provisioned seeds, equipped, let free

Scatter themselves in dry and prosperous noons
By floaters, parachutes and by balloons;
Shoot forth from pods by little traps and springs,
Or fall with hooks to cling, or fly with wings;
Or with the rolling bush, far driven by the wind,
Forsake old haunts and farther meadows find;
Or by their sweet investitures of flesh
Enslave the unconscious birds
To carry them and plant their life afresh—
This is the equal course of man who girds
His days with labor and with stores of food.

ORMUND

But yet his thought moves in a higher mood;
It strives to plant with wisdom and with words,
By the same Urge unconquerable which frees
And moves the pod and thistle and the grape,
And the bush that rolls before the autumn breeze.
Man stood erect and left behind the ape
By the same Genius moving the humblest weed.
Why should the Genius stop, once having shown
Dreams of a higher life than man has known?
Flowerings will be of the provisioned seed
Of aspiration for completer life;
Flowerings of hunger for delight more deep;
And more ascents for man who out of strife,
Hate, ignorance, error, war and storm
Of living, kept his aspiration warm,
And treasured great awakenings in the sleep
Of the creative hope which wrought
His dust to dreams, to restless thought.

What! Shall the Genius stay him now, nor lift
His life to higher planes, when from the cells
Of single mooded life it won the gift
Of thought and passion, and the miracles
Of starry contemplation, where it dwells
At work? but not defeated or adrift!

ARIMANIUS

The war is over. Thousands under earth
Where the plain rolls, and where the mountain slopes
Make lush the spring. But if their hopes give birth
To liberties and these again to hopes,
And on and on repeating their increase
Of death in war, and life renewed in peace,
None has the profit of the thing he sowed—
What are such riches to a soul in pain?
What wealth to him who walks before the goad?
What is it if you cannot use the gain
Inherited? What is the gain with Lee?
The millenium, if it come, is far away.
The war will crop in small moralities,
And thus its small paternity betray.
The toper, gambler, those who love and play,
The Sabbath breakers, with the liberties
Of new born Henrys, Franklins, will decay.
Business, the criminal, will make a crime,
And crime alone of what impedes his sway.
This war was waged by Business, and the time
Is here of those who tax and rob—but pray!

ORMUND

You talk at times just like a mortal man.
There's work for us to do at Powhatan.
Lee rouses and the Destiny will obey.

(*The scene closes.*)

Scene 3: Beside a farmer's house in Powhatan county,
        Virginia. Ormund and Arimanius.

ORMUND

We will await his waking, then attend
His journey into Lexington to the end.

ARIMANIUS

Yes, if there were some way to help, befriend.

ORMUND

Whisper him secrets that he may not break,
And what he was and what he is forsake.
Keep himself visioned that he may not pass
From the oak he is to rag weed or sand grass.
Keep him in mind of what he has desired;
And how he felt, believed, and how aspired,
And what he chose, rejected, loved and why;
Help him endure the storm dust rolling by.
Let not the false opinion of the crowd
Corrupt his self-esteem till disendowed
The hatred of the mob, and its dispraise
Make him a broken creature of small days—
Keep him himself and in his duty proud.

ARIMANIUS

I shall.   And you my brother?

ORMUND
                    I have vowed.

Scene 4: A room in the farmer's house.   A young soldier;
        a farmer.

FARMER

It's four o'clock.   How sound the General sleeps.
Don't wake him up.

SOLDIER
        I shan't.

FARMER
                        Don't go to-day;
Wait till to-morrow morning, when it's cool,
And let him sleep.   This August heat's too much
For travel.

SOLDIER
            But there is a moon to-night,
And the evening air out of the hills will blow.

FARMER

How much he sleeps!

SOLDIER
                        He never will make up
The wakefulness of Gettysburg and Richmond,
And all those years of watching.   Some forget
He was not young in sixty-one, nor young
Last April in the Wilderness.

FARMER
                                    Now he grieves.
The story is about this neighborhood
That when at Appomattox—Appomattox—
He signed the peace with Grant, he just rose up
And left the room.   But when he looked and saw
Virginia's hills, . . . Virginia's hills—good Lord,
I cry just like a woman—when he saw
Virginia's hills, he struck his hands together
Like a man does too hurt to say a word;
Then mounted Traveler and rode away.

SOLDIER
I saw it, and it's true.   But all the rest
Who didn't know that he had made the peace,
And thought he'd call a battle, waiting there,
Crowded around him when he rode, and cried,
And kneeled to him, and begged him shedding tears
To fight again and wipe away defeat,
Or losing let them die and so forget.
He wouldn't.   For he has no little spite,
And what was more he loved us, and his heart
Was like a father's when he saw us there,
A little band of tattered, broken men
Ready to charge, but what a foe to charge!
They stripped their lines, and showed us how they stood,
Legion on legion back of legion, legions,
Like thickets back of thickets, all of steel.
This was before he sent the flag of truce.
We didn't know it and we meant to trample
The thickets, if we could.

FARMER

Well, he was right.
It would have been a stubborn hate and murder. . . .
Where is that Englishman who was coming back?

SOLDIER

That's ended.   He will not return.

FARMER

Why not?
They say that Oxford is the biggest school
In England, and to teach the English war
Would bring the General honor, peace and wealth.

SOLDIER

But leave us in the lurch—or so he thinks.

FARMER

Well, but they'll pile their meanness on to him.
He is the head and we are but the tail;
They'll pile their hatred, slander on to him.
They're going to drag him into court, they say,
And try him like a criminal for the war,
As old John Brown was tried for Harper's Ferry;
And maybe like John Brown they'll hang him too.
The North has whipped us and the North intends
To rob us and to rule us—we can stand it.
But I don't like to see the General
Insulted and abused and made a shame

For old John Brown, the North, or anything.
And so I wish he'd go to England, get
Up and away from this.   He's pretty old;
He's pretty broken, for his heart is broken.

SOLDIER

When he awakes we start for Lexington.

FARMER

What?

SOLDIER

        To head the college.   Why, you heard him say
He had a task he wouldn't shirk for gold,
Or peace, or ease, or honor?

FARMER

                        Yes, I heard him.

SOLDIER

He meant it.   And we go to Lexington.

FARMER

To teach that school?

SOLDIER

                Founded by Washington.
Because he loves Virginia, and her youth;
Because he led a war that failed, and now
His life belongs to those who followed failure.
Because he means to start and from the bottom
Build up these broken youths to some success.

FARMER

So that's the way?

SOLDIER

That Englishman was gone
About an hour—and you were in the field—
When the committee sent from Lexington,
Looking so funny in their borrowed suits,
Arrived here, begging him to be the head
Of the college there.

FARMER

And so he took the job?

SOLDIER

He didn't take it, and he didn't refuse it.
He told them he was doubtful of the good
His leadership would do the school.

FARMER

Well, but—

If England is so keen to have him why
Should he have doubts about this little school?

SOLDIER

His name you know, his name, his reputation.

FARMER

Name—what?

SOLDIER

Yes, made another word, you know
For rebel, traitor, which he feared would hurt
The school, the boys.

FARMER

No, never in the South.

SOLDIER

Don't be so sure.   Some think he might have won;
Some blame him still for Gettysburg; and some
Wish he had fought till whipped; and others hate
The war's beginning, some the war as fought.
Remember how in Richmond all were glad
The city fell, even the whites were grateful
Beside the happy niggers, who danced and sang.
Why, Lincoln walked the drunken streets of Richmond
With only ten marines to keep him guard,
And wasn't stayed or spoken to at all;
But had the silence, maybe the admiration
Of citizens, of gamblers, toughs and drunks.
I say it's wonderful.   I say that something
Beside our guns were silenced—yes, our faith,
Our Southern pride are silenced, and are gone.
I say that Cæsar in no conquered city
Entered the palace of a flying king
So unattended as Abe Lincoln walked
Into the White House of the Southern States;
Nor sat upon the throne as Lincoln teetered
In Davis's chair still with its bottom warm.
It's wonderful. . . .   And so he hesitated
To think about the good that he could do,
And whether that would overcome the hurt
His name might bring the school of Lexington.
He's thought it out.   He's going.   There, he stirs!

FARMER

He is awake.   Wait!   General!   Is there something?
(*Goes to Lee's door and raps softly.*)

LEE (*within*)

Just saddle Traveler.   I'm going now.

(*Lee enters.*)

I must be on my way.

FARMER

It's pretty hot.
I wish you'd wait till evening.

LEE

I must be on my way.   Evening's soon.

SOLDIER

May I go with you?

LEE

No need for that.   Go to your home, my son.
Go to your home.   Take up and build anew
The life you left for me and for the South.
Your duty is to live, and mine to live.
Forget the hatred of the war and be
Not a Virginian only, but being that
A new American, and transmit the pride
To your sons to be, that a new America
Be yours and theirs.   This is my work and yours.

SOLDIER

I promise, General, to try—I promise.

LEE

So shall we heal our country.   And may God
Protect and save you, son.

SOLDIER

I promise—still
I wish I'd died at Gettysburg. I don't
Want to see what I see.

LEE

Farewell.

SOLDIER

Farewell.

(*Lee goes out with the farmer.   The soldier stands at the
door.*)

SOLDIER

So ends our hope.   So ends our battle faith;
So is our army dwindled to this man,
This lonely horseman off to Lexington
To teach a school.   I wish to God I'd died
At Gettysburg.   I almost wish a bullet
Had taken him at Gettysburg. . . .   Who are those
Two fellows in the road who wait for him?
No, what's the matter with me?   Streaks of light!
Looked like two soldiers uniformed in gray—
Maybe he didn't want me, having them.
'Twas nothing, nothing but the sunlight shining
Before my eyes a little blurred—a little.
He's in the road now.   My, how straight he sits.
I see his white hair toying with the wind.

He's going down the hill now—well, good bye—
A last farewell—I swear two soldiers walk
On either side of Traveler—no, I'm fooled.
Good bye, you have your troubles, so have I.
Trouble is measured by the man who has it—
I'm just a common soldier, you're a god.
Go to my home!   I haven't any.   Well,
Go make a home.   I'm like the General,
I lost the Arlington I had.   The South
Has lost its Arlington.   What's left to do
But carry brick, and dig, and saw and lift?

Scene 5:   Lee riding Traveler on the way to Lexington;
Ormund and Arimanius walk at either side.   The
Blue Ridge mountains are in view; and the
little city at last.   Lee talks out his meditations to Traveler.

LEE

Traveler!   Do you understand this day
That has come to pass?
The stillness of these fields, these woods
Is it not mine, and being mine not yours?
Faithfulest friend!   Who lives through me,
Lives in my thoughts and feels through me;
Yielding your swiftness which I needed in war,
And the strength above a man's
Found in you, which you gave
As if you knew.   And in that work became
My body and my mind, as I had been
One body with you.

Traveler!   No more the bursting shell!
No more the thunder of the guns,
And the terrible beauty of battle
Which you beheld, in key with me,
With neck so proudly arched and nostrils wide
To inhale the smoke of fury.
Trusted Traveler!   Spirit alert to war!
Step after step, mile after mile you bear me
As if you knew, as if you grieved,
As if you asked me, why this silent way,
This day of a leisured journey,
And not the haste of the old days
Toward the sound of commencing battle.
As I ask God to show this day,
And trust Him to reveal it or withhold it,
So you trust me to direct your steps,
Toward what I seek, and what in your devotion
Is what you seek as well.
Faithful Traveler!   Nearest of friends at last!
Do you remember how I came to you
Last midnight, put my arms about your neck,
And drew you to me?
I was lonely Traveler, waking at midnight with these
        griefs,
Which will not die.
If all your days of glory are behind,
And the pride of momentous service is no more;
And the battle is lost, and nothing left for you
But the canter on the hills to give me strength,
To lift the youth I led to life again,
Does anything remain to me but Duty,

Quietly done, as patiently you await
The hour of my mount for health, well to fulfill
The task imposed by Fate?
So you remain a part of me, and give
Your mind to mine, your body to my body
To the ends of Wisdom and Peace, as in the war
You were wings to my feet.
Traveler!   What is our home to be?
But never a home again like Arlington!
There lies our home amid the quiet hills
Of Lexington, and back of us our lost,
Our ruined home, never to be regained,
Never regained, my Traveler, never regained!
All that I had of lands, of comforts lost.
Nothing is left but you—but you are not
A property, but a soul, almost my flesh,
As my wife and children are. . . .
And saving these all things are swept away;
And I am stripped, made naked to the world!
Yes! and the loss of comrades, cruelly struck
From the lists of life!
And as for those who live, shall we resume
In reminiscence, days and loves that were,
And escape the espionage,
Which sees us the defeated, as traitors too
In memories of rebellion?
No, though our faith remains in the lost cause,
And no shame has accrued for what we did,
Still for a space 'tis fitting not to meet.
And so great loneliness must be my portion,
Companioned only by incessant thoughts,

And memories, and dreams in slumber and awake,
From which my soul shall start with battle words:
"Forward!" or "Strike the Tent!"
As it has been these weeks of hunted rest. . . .
Then as to honor, is it lost as well?
No! As the rock I stand against the thought
With which the North would break me, if convinced
That I had played the traitor.
Not those who make my captaincy a crime,
And drag my sword before a magistrate,
To weigh it in the scales of an assize—
Not these shall touch my honor, for I will to stand
With my forbears, who made this Nation first,
And with my kinsman Washington.
And I will show my cause and soul so fair
By duty done, and full acceptance lived
Of the arbitrament of war, that all shall see
What I strove to do, and what I am.
Duty! Daily and faithfully done!
O, Thou great God! Whose presence I closely feel
Around this soaring sky, these eternal hills,
Sustain me, and support, and build again
This broken land. And save it from the curse
That follows war, and from the ruinous creed
Which fired the subtle faction of the North
To make this realm of free, confederate states
One merged and vast republic,
Warlike abroad and tyrannous at home;
To which the township, county and the state
Shall be as satrapies, and a central power,
Reckless of liberty, shall play the despot!

Be not my labor lost, but be my fate,
My destitution and my sacrifice,
For the rights of men, protected by the reserved
Rights of a local sovereignty, the seeds
Of liberty renewed, and a new Virginia,
A South restored, and a North more free.
And if I failed to vindicate a realm
Of a new freedom, may the olden realm
Thrive with the freedom we designed
In waging war!
Be the righteousness in which I judged,
And drew my sword, the inheritable life
Of what I did, and led these youths to do,
From Charlottesville and Lexington;
And the hate of our love be but the sheathing flesh,
Ensuring the life, and the safety of the seed
Of our intent, and its prosperous scattering.
So that by the miracle of creation,
Which works no less in souls than in fields of corn,
Love may emerge, and grow from Hate and Waste,
And sweeten the land with light!
What though we asked for nothing but the Union
As our fathers had made it;
What though we fought against a Force that changed it;
What though we judged the war was brought to us,
And was never fated, and needed not to be;
What though our proffered compromise, in pride
And power rejected had prevented war, if met
In the spirit of our spirit, and we warred
For peace and found it not till we were broken—
Were not our judgments set aside by Thee,

And all our great disaster willed of Thee?
For all this soaring sky, and these slumbering hills,
Symbols of Time and of Eternity
Quiet our griefs, as a mother stills her child,
And soothe us with belief that all is good.
Nothing is left to man but his intent
Made pure by conscience, wisdom and ceaseless thought,
Along the ways of life, where he must stray,
But straying find the path again, or show
By his missteps the way to other feet,
While the star of Duty shines,
To guide or to betray,
As eyes perceive the star.
So is the soul of man enlarged and lifted
The while it errs,
Still favored as the flower of flowers!

                (*He comes nearer Lexington.*)

Blue Hills beyond this little town of spires
Receive me now!
And the white columns of these halls receive me,
Hallowed by him whose great munificience
Established them above this winding river,
And let them bear his name!
What happier fate
Were mine, than after war to enter
Here, where his name inspires me
To rebuild, until the love of God
Spread from this center to the farthest North,
And East and West, till it become a shrine
Of Liberty and Peace, and what was never
Done by hate, nor force nor war,

Be done by love and service, the secret forces
Hidden from captains and revealed to children?
Traveler! There lies our place of duty,
Our home, and even our tombs at last
Sepulchered by these hills.
Glad shouts arise to welcome us,
You my warrior-steed who bear,
And me the lonely rider.

> (*Lee rides into the narrow streets of Lexington, surrounded
> by throngs of men, women and children, who are singing
> and rejoicing in homage of his arrival. Ormund and
> Arimanius walk beside Traveler unseen.*)

ARIMANIUS

Here where songs are and where the banners flap,
Where votive flowers are strewn along his path,
As it were to hide his sorrow's handicap,
Still I perceive the Republic's rising wrath
Laughing to see him enter in the trap.

ORMUND

What trap?

ARIMANIUS

                Why this! Horse Mountain, yonder river,
These hills the symbol of advancing walls
Pressing around him closer terminals
Of living, as the jailer and lawgiver
Fate feeds him crusts until his spirit falls.
The little days to be will suffocate him
With narrowing life until they immolate him.

The World Spirit now at last has deified
Brown's insurrection, cursing it in Lee.
False Spirit, changing into fratricide
That which was once a war for Liberty.
False Spirit! Giving once the principle
And precedent of revolution, then
When later used, to curse it into hell—
O, passionate, seeking, but misguided men!
To Germans, Continentals, émigrés
What but a servant was state sovereignty?
So to the master did they part the ways,
The master, national democracy!
Master indeed, and despot will it be;
And all as slaves their aching knees will bend;
The western farms will rule the eastern town;
Councils, assemblies, governors will attend
The imperial bigotry of old John Brown,
Miscalled the Union to defeat the South.
The Union was a mask upon the face
Of Business, kissing with a Judas mouth
The Liberty it tricked with an embrace.
Against this Titan bully, ironmonger,
Lee crumpled with his Athens nourished boys.
Look! The World Spirit ever brings to hunger
The soul whom God or Liberty decoys.

ORMUND

You talk as if you thought that kings were blest.
All have defeat that eats away the breast.
Neither the Spirit, Nature, says, go live;
Both watch to see that men are forced to give.

Death hinders not the gift, but speeds it faster;
Dishonor brightens it for the faithful souled.
There is a treasury of the Nation vaster
Than chests of steel that keep the Nation's gold.
Into its richness Lincoln, Lee have paid
Their tributes from a life devoted store.
What they have done by Time will be assayed,
Nor shall it vanish at a rifled door.
Here losing life for duty made his master,
Lee shall find life, and find it more and more.

ARIMANIUS

Meanwhile there's Envy which can never rest
Till honor from a man is dispossessed.
Lee must be laid to earth both trunk and bough . . .
Above this scene of gayety, this orchestic
Rejoicing once again I see the brow
Of the Republic angry and majestic.
She comes to Lexington to pronounce her vow—
Let us stand near her, let us hear her now.

(The scene closes.)

ACT FOUR

Scene: The campus of Washington University, Lexington, Virginia. Ormund, Arimanius, The Republic, The South, Virginia, A Messenger.

THE REPUBLIC

From wandering through my obedient domain
Far as my pious East is to the sea
Which waters the mountain slopes beyond the plain
Of Kansas and Nebraska, rendered free
By my insuperable will, and by my sword,
I come to look again upon the land
Which I forewarned against the idiot course
Of riotous defiance to my command,
And failed as I foresaw, and so foretold,
With all this consequence of righteous force,
Which Justice and the laws of God behold,
Visited upon rebellion, and with hate,
Ruin and hunger flocking to pick clean
The bones of vanquished men! So be the fate
Of these, this South, a warning ever seen
Of futures, against resistance to the law.
As it was said: If God wills all the wealth
Piled by the bondsman for two hundred years
Of unrequited toil, be sunk, and the sword
Pay drop for drop, for every drop of blood
Drawn by the lash . . . so be disaster's flood

119

To you, O South! The judgments of the Lord
Are true, and so have stood;
And they are righteous altogether, and have swept
Your land with flame, and cast your mighty down.
So I have loosed rejoicings, which were kept
Restrained at Appomattox, and have reversed
The words, Let us have Peace, that I might crown
Defeat with ignominy; and I have cursed
The soul of Lee with the martyred soul of Brown,
To hunt him like a bloodhound, and avenge
The shame of Harper's Ferry, which rejoiced
Your Lee to captain! Now my North rejoices;
And God's great retribution, many voiced,
In righteous anger lashes through the voices
Of Sumner and of Stevens, and summons pride
To witness Lee's rebellion swallowed up
In Brown's rebellion, and his flesh that died,
Become your death, and his briefest cup your cup,
These five years drained to the poisonous dregs of woe!
Lee I have made a felon, by my grace—
Which is my hatred thrice refined—
Enlarged of prison bars, but better prisoned
In a little task and life amid these hills,
Whose pathos and whose silence will unbind
Tormenting memories, as his soul is visioned
In hours of nothingness to see the ills
He wrought against the law, himself as well!
And to the end of order, and a peace
Never to be imperilled more, I carved
The Southern States in districts, better to quell
The sullen heart, where a broken people starved,

And tugged the iron wristlets, which were slipped
From black to white; until the southern knees
Bend to my Instrument of Rule, equipped
With powers imperial as to civil rights,
The negro ballot!

THE SOUTH

So a foe who fights
By laws of War in honor, shall not be
Accorded terms befitting such a foe?

THE REPUBLIC

It was not war, but a vile conspiracy,
A foul rebellion. And in Fort Monroe
Your Davis still should fester.

THE SOUTH

We misread
Your purpose, and so failed to estimate
The bitterness and largeness of your hate.

THE REPUBLIC

Not hate for you, but justice to our dead.

THE SOUTH

Appeal not to your dead, who were but those
Who fed and nursed us at the battle's close;
Who took our hands as foeman worthy of
Their swords, and later worthy of their love.
Good champions strive for mastery, and frown
To strike the unlucky challenger when down.

Now you should treat me as a man who made
A valiant struggle, bringing great renown
To you who mastered me, and not degrade
Your victory with mocks and missiles thrown.
You warred to free the slave. Now he is freed,
And I accept the verdict; and what need
Of these indignities, and martial law,
Save that you plan what Jefferson foresaw:
Your purpose to submerge the confederate
Love of the states with hate imperial?
You took us by the hand to signify
Your admiration, now you give the lie
To that fine chivalry, by treating us
As evil doers, not as valorous
Contenders with the sword! And this you do
With moralistic clamor, calls to God
To punish us as wicked souls, untrue,
Through you rewarded with the righteous rod,
With which to scourge us! Shall we teach our youth
To read the Book, we both invoked, as chants
Of double meaning, always masked as truth?
Invoked in battle, and by militants
For God, and when the peace comes still perused
For words wherewith to put aside the peace
Good will and amnesty for wrong excused,
If we have wronged you, which it teaches too?
So making it in war a battle cry,
And after war a code for rulers who
Glean battle-fields for treasure, and who pick
The pockets of the slain, and enter where
Want, Infancy, and Sorrow nurse the sick,

To gather taxes for the sword you bear
After our forced submission, and the Truce
Which we requested and you made?

VIRGINIA

War may assume the name of Law or Right,
Or Justice, seeking to effectuate
Its purpose, in the maddened masquerade
Of the sons of thunder, Pride and Hate,
Where Thought is overcome by Might.
Seeing my stricken land, my dying Lee
I almost feel it had been best
If we had not resisted your great wrong
In making war upon us.

THE REPUBLIC

Liberty

Has risen from the flames!

VIRGINIA

For whom?   The strong!
And, as of old new tyrannies attest
The folly of a liberty war attained.
Whatever be the way, revenge and wrath
Must still corrupt the life which they have stained
With violence and its bitter aftermath!

THE REPUBLIC

'Twere better you had acted on these truths.

VIRGINIA

We strove to act upon them, but the sleuths
Of envy and material dominance,
Forever on the scent of trade, and rule
Of traffic, yelped the war, and would not chance
The loss of game in peace.

THE REPUBLIC

You still befool
Your minds with reasonings as weak as these.

VIRGINIA

Did we not stay our swords and offer peace?

THE REPUBLIC

Peace with your will to leave me, so rebel!

VIRGINIA

But if the Union be inviolable,
And states may not secede, and so impair
Your firm integrity, how may you now
Exclude me from the Union, yet avow
The sophistry of a Union, where the rights
Of states are trampled, over which you bear
Your Roman sovereignty? How may there be
A Union without states, or liberty
In either, save it be in both; or you
Be indestructible with me destroyed?
For I must be as deathless as you are,
Or both of us must die. And in the war,

And now in peace, your hatred has employed
The means of dissolution, and you do
What you killed us for doing!

THE REPUBLIC
Never true!

THE SOUTH
Yes, for you keep us from you, who averred
We had no right to leave you.

THE REPUBLIC
I have heard
Your Lee has spoken so.

VIRGINIA
Now answer him!
You struck his sword from hand, but not his word
Shall you strike out of memory, or dim.
Who has destroyed the Union, we who sought
In vain to leave it, or your hate which locks
The door of our return? We who declined
The spurious love which said we could not leave;
Or we who stand without, whose hand still knocks
Upon the door of the unforgiving mind?
Who has destroyed the Union, we who grieve
Shut out to desolation, amid the mocks
Of your triumphant strength, whose heel
Tramped Maryland, and now is on our neck,
Forbidding us to rise, or you whose weal
Must perish in our wreck?

THE REPUBLIC

You never left the Union but as one
Who for a time deserts his home, but still
Cannot dissever the strains of blood which run
In unity against his petulant will.
You shall return at last and be received
By me whom you dishonored and aggrieved.

THE SOUTH

Let it be soon, for till it be
No Union is in this disunity.

THE REPUBLIC

A new day dawns! And these days shall become
As a flood which passes, and men build again;
And fields are harvested, and gardens bloom;
And cities are rebuilded, and the plain
Of the remotest places teem with men
Whose sunburnt arms shall gather grain,
Where once impassable grasses fed wild cattle.
My breast healed of these wounds shall stir
With richer life, and the thunderings of battle
Shall be as stories told by the evening fire,
And your woes be as if they never were.
I shall be as a soul whose false desire
Is forgotten in remembrance of its good,
And its essential nature, and its deeds.
And from the stern devotion, fortitude
Of all my sons, and from blossoms, even weeds
I shall extract the cordial of my strength.

Whatever I have done, by what inept
And muddling course, I have expunged at length
The spot of slavery; and I have kept
The promise of my nature, though it break
Some faith, as you would term it. We are still
Men who are weak, and so forsake
In blindness, or in will
The path, but there are powers who make
Destiny and a goodness out of ill!

VIRGINIA

So if it be, your head must yet be bowed
To honor Lee, and you must bend your pride
To recognize his glory, and be proud
To change your hate to love, that he may be
Your son at last. For he were less than Lee
If he besought your favor, or became,
To win it, recreant to his fame.
You must repent your bitterness, not impose
His vision's recantation as the price
Of love renewed, lest with the passing throes
Of war his vision come to you, or you perceive
Warrant for honor in the sacrifice
He made for Duty, and seeing your hands weave
A wreath for his dishonored head at last.
You shall be rich in lands, even to the tides
Of severed oceans, and in cities great,
And gold mined from the mountain sides;
And powerful in war. But what shall last
When Time cries down a Nation's high estate
Of ships and cities, save the souls who gave

To Time a glory by the gift of Truth,
Or Duty, Courage, Sacrifice, or Thought;
And who in patience suffering the ruth
Of the passing hour, died in an ignorant land
To make the whole wide earth their grave?
Man is a spirit! But cities are of earth,
Raised by man's spirit, and to earth return.
But what is of the spirit, that remains
To sow anew, and bring a richer birth.
By thought the ship is builded, and the plains
Subdued and harvested. But misfortunes borne
Nobly and so accepted as a good,
Is thought that builds the soul, and gives to Time
A richness beyond gold, for the brotherhood
Of men to live by. This was Lee, whose soul
Shone in defeat to guide us, and who strove
To heal, and called to us to shun
Our local hates and faiths, and to enroll
Our sons as once again Americans.
You cannot well disown so great a son!

THE REPUBLIC

Whatever be his mind, or my intent
Toward his future, this has gladdened me:
Your people labor to restore content,
And bring again the land's prosperity.

VIRGINIA

To see this, lifted from the heart of Lee
Great doubt and sorrow too.

THE REPUBLIC

And well it should,

Seeing that he was the potential cause
Of this momentous breaking of my laws.

VIRGINIA

Out of these halls consider what a flood
Of passionate spirits poured, and not alone
These and the southern schools, but north as well:
Princeton, from whence my Lighthorse Harry came
To revolution against a rejected throne,
Sustained me and enlarged my battle flame,
Kindled by Lexington and Charlottesville,
Who neither for blood lust, hate nor trophies fought;
But as a Christian should for viable
Friendship and peace thereafter to be wrought;
By whom dirt, fasting, wounds and death were thought
God's glory and an honor end of life.
Time shall remember the remorseless odds
They struggled with, but I shall shout along
The valleys and hills of history, until God's
Will shall listen to mine to undo the wrong
You do them, and their spirits shall mount and ride
The wings of legend and persuasive song:
These boys whose spirits sparkled, and whose wit
Flashed in the dark, the drifting rain, the sleet;
Whom hunger, and whom thirst could not depress;
Who kept their spirits clear and infinite
In strength above the flesh's weariness;
Who gay of heart surrendered the great gift
Of life in youth. And as the sentry Death

Challenged them one by one, smiled undismayed,
And entered captive the ranks of ended breath.
Oh, you shall honor them at last, and crown
With memory their leader, who put by
Honors and wealth to train them, whom he led
Through war, in peace to duty, and to frown
Upon remembrance of their tragedy,
And of your violence and strength, which sped
The ruin of their land. These five long years,
About these halls accessible and wise
Has he uplifted hopes, and quieted fears,
And counseled, labored in this enterprise
Of life re-made, with failing health to stay
His spirit, and with memories to assail
His resolution. For the eagle caged
Dreams of the peaks 'round which the lightnings play;
And you have been a taunter before his jail,
And spoken detraction of the war he waged.
Until through care and labor, sleepless grief
For seeing his sons in cheerfulness of mood
Strive for recapture of the ways of life,
And for new happiness, and for relief
From wounds, and from the bitterness of strife,
His master soul, though breathing faithful prayers,
And hidden in the tenderness of Christ,
Has grown beyond the body, and its cares;
And he has fallen and is sacrificed
In the mystery of these days.

MESSENGER

Yes, fallen indeed!

VIRGINIA

What emphasis is this?

MESSENGER

Our Lee is dead.

VIRGINIA

How has death touched that white and sovereign head?

MESSENGER

With weariness from a heart that would not heed
The warnings of its age, and which was spent;
But with a soul erect, unconquered,
He died and dying whispered, "Strike the tent!"

VIRGINIA

Now let me stand a moment by his bier,
Proud in my sorrow, shaken, but no tear.

ARIMANIUS

Let us stand too, silent and reverent.

ORMUND

He was a soul of any soul the peer.

ARIMANIUS

They bear him now with dirges.   Let us hear.

(The scene closes.)

Scene 2: The funeral procession on the campus of the
University.

DIRGE OF STUDENTS

I

1

Let the bells toll, then let the bells be still
As we bury the captain of our broken arms,
Before the guns roar and the bugles shrill,
And wake the valleys with alarms.
Toll now the bells high in the swaying steeples
To the time of our martial feet.
We who are pale, we who are silent lipped
Shall bear our captain amid uncovered peoples
To the eternal silence of the crypt,
Our captain who made victory of defeat.
But ere our captain's body enter the dark,
And the marble door be sealed,
Let the throng pass,
Let woman, boy and man, and veteran pass,
One by one, one by one, let all who loved him pass,
And look upon this face, this patriarch
Of the lineage of the heroic battle-field,
Whom war o'erthrew, whom life gave victory.

2

For the last let all who loved him look upon
This brow and breast to marble turned;
These hands upon his breast that now have won
The peace for which he yearned.

This brow full, high and clear,
Where thronged his vision, conscience, tenderness;
This breast that never harbored fear,
But stirred alone with nobleness.
Over him let the mantle lie,
As if thrown over him for fitful sleep
Between the midnight and the dawn, between
The hoot of the owl, the gray of the dawning sky:
Even as it covered him in the Wilderness,
Sleeping beside us, whom he called his boys,
Grieving for us, and for the unforeseen
Day of the battle. Or as it lay upon him
Couched by his twin, the fiery son
These years asleep in Lexington,
Since quick disaster won him—
The flame of the Shenandoah quenched ere it could run
Its course with him who lies here, and who failed
Because that sun-lit sword was hurled
From the dauntless hand that bore it,
Before the rapt eyes of a wondering world!
So couch him now, and by his bier
To speak his victory and our loss,
Against the gray that shrouds him here,
Place the black cross:
Eternal symbol of man's life;
Eternal symbol of its end;
Man's soul that climbs amid unmeaning strife,
And cannot rest, but must ascend
Amid disaster and departed friend
To the hill-top's desolate goal,
Where the victory is not of flesh or guns,

But of the soul,
Poured out in death to save and recreate
By the strength of a visioned truth
A people from bitterness and hate,
And strife, which would perpetuate
Division upon the Nation's rising youth.
So lies he here who gave himself
In fullest measure to his land.
Let the bells cease as round this bier you stand;
Let silence be as of the hills;
Let no heart be unmanned.
The Fate which prospers and fulfills
Has not withdrawn His hand.
Let your thoughts be as a cloud which wills
Its way where no rain drops;
And be your sorrow as the evening sun
Upon the mountain tops!

II

This is our friend, our father who is so still,
Who sleeps and wakens not.
Here lies the scion of that Launcelot
Who triumphed because a better sword was wrought
Out of the iron art of Hastings' day:
As our captain fell before the cunning of the mill,
To which his soul opposed the brighter flame
Of the blood that bore his name.
Here lies he whom no skill,
Nor faith, nor prayers, nor will
Served for the victory, or to stay
The artisans of steel,

Who left behind the anvil, which we kept;
The bellows and the water wheel,
And the mountain forge beside the spinning reel,
And seized for slaves the piston and the blast.
These genii rose against him thick as clouds
That storm a star, whose splendor overcast
Abides the calm of heaven, for men to see.
Giant embattled and overcome
By these and by our past,
He was victorious, no less, at last,
By the soul, which tempers souls, and leaves to flesh
The tempering of swords.
We are at fault, our fathers too have sinned
Against the age, and we must recompense
The new day, which upon this mighty wind
Of war announced its immanence,
By rising to the spirit of this hour,
As he did, and so master it and live
Through Duty and through sacrifice;
Forgiving what he taught us to forgive,
That the land he loved may burst to fuller flower!

III

Now ere our captain's body enter the dark,
And the marble door be sealed
With iron clasps inwrought,
Let the throngs pass,
Let woman, boy and man and veteran pass,
One by one, one by one . . . let all who loved him pass,
Of the lineage of the battle-field of Thought.
To the tolling of bells, and the measured tread

Of us who followed him in war;
Of us who follow him to live,
Let the body of him be borne, our sacred dead.
Bring, too, his Traveler, riderless forever,
To help us bear our vanquished conquerer,
His faithful horse, that crossed the perilous river,
And on the battle lines,
Where the shell bursts, and the bullet whines,
Bore him, whom he shall bear no more,
Save to the chapel door,
And the sunless crypt beneath!
Carry for him our tattered flags
Torn by the ravenous teeth
Of shot that hunted up the inaccessible crags,
And made our meadows barren as a heath.
Like him they sleep!   They shall not be
In war again unfurled.
But new made banners of the free
Shall lead a restless world,
To vindicate the soul of Lee,
Till freedom rule the world!

IV

Flags and bodies of men are for the dust.
Captains withdraw to death, and swords
Dull and crumble with rust,
With the fallen cause which humbles them.
But the living air of life calls into being
Swords sharper, even as it crumbles them
By the spirit of creation and decay.
Hence if this Nation newly made

Through our defeat and sorrow,
Fatten with spoils and trade;
And the promise of to-day's to-morrow
Dishonor him and us, and shame
Our confidence . . . be man's revolt again
By his immortal spirit led,
Which cannot otherwise be honored,
Nor liberty subserved save by such wills . . .
But now as round the crypt we stand,
Let silence be as of the hills.
Let no heart be unmanned.
The Fate that prospers and fulfills
Will not withdraw His hand!

V

Come, great victorious North
And grieve with us
For our great dead, who is your dead!
Come plowmen from the West whose arms are swarth;
Come arrogant New England, and henceforth
Consider him, though you believe with us
Never, by interest and revenge misled.
He was the whole land's friend:
He gave devotion to the South,
And to the faith of state vitality;
But falling, he arose, and to the end
Gave love to man, and to the whole wide land
For union and for greater liberty.
Our loss of him is yours, come near and stand
While we entomb the heart that beat
Close to the God of love, not God of justice, power.

Out of his sacrifice and his defeat
Has come a treasure, leaving incomplete
Your greatness, O, Republic, if you blind
Your eyes against it.   None,
Neither your Lincoln, nor the Washington
We both revere has given more
To build, to brighten, and to bind
Your fame with splendor to the end of time.
Now close the marble door
With iron clasps inwrought,
While we return to the duty that he taught.

VI

O, empty autumnal sky of the flying leaf!
This great white face that seemed to wear
The sorrow of a Nation, and the grief
Of a whole people seemed to bear,
Is hidden in the tomb, and soon shall fare
To dust and lose the mould
Of suffering and care.
So may our sorrow fade, and the manifold
Tragedy of war sink like his frame,
To spring in life again
With the splendor of his fame!

VOICES

No grief for the great ones whose labor is ended,
Who pass from our seeing through doors that are sealed;
Made safe from all danger, by distance defended,
Sepultured in silence they sleep and are healed,

What's a future of bugles, the hills of hereafter,
Where trenches are guarding the captains who sleep?
They dream with the Aprils whose rivulet laughter
Is faint amid grasses on valley and steep.

They have willed you the world, be the trust still evaded
Their rebuke is the quiet, the light of the stars.
They watch as a Truth on a race unpersuaded;
They rule as a Vision that smiles at the wars.

Their realm is dominion of wisdom through living.
They live and they die not through wisdom bequeathed.
They are changed to immortals, relentless, forgiving.
They are swords in the light of eternity sheathed.

Day dawns! The New Age is arisen!
They who wept shall sing.
The mourning of the slave shall bring a vision,
And the music of an unknown string.
Nothing is at the core of being but the measure
Of music, nothing in wars, or silence, laws;
The world is but a pipe whose toil or leisure
Obeys great fingers making the pitch and pause.
The New Age moves more freely and around
The magic of a more melodious sound!

THE END